Number 16 Winter '75

Cover and interior graphics taken from Jorge Enciso's *Designs from Pre-Columbian Mexico, Dover,* **1971. Sr. Enciso selected and executed all the designs for the book from the surfaces of** *malacates* **or spindle whorls, small baked-clay receptacles with a circular hole in the center.** *Malacates* **are commonly found in archeological sites ranging from the most ancient period up to the era of the Conquest.**

Photo credits: Page 4, Vicenzo Flore: page 69, Jerry Bauer.

Editor	*Editorial Assistants*
Ronald Christ	Robin Burke
Associate Editor	Gregory Kolovakos
Rosario Santos	Pamela Zapata
Consulting Editor	*Advisory Board*
Emir Rodríguez Monegal	Leopoldo Castedo
Advisory Editors	José Guillermo Castillo
Thomas Colchie	Zunilda Gertel
Alexander Coleman	Victoria Ocampo
	José Miguel Oviedo

A publication of the Center for Inter-American Relations
The Center, a non-profit, tax-exempt, membership corporation financed by foundation support, membership dues and corporate and individual gifts, conducts educational programs in the visual and performing arts, literature and public affairs.

 FOCUS

JUAN CARLOS ONETTI'S

A Brief Life

Translated by Hortense Carpentier
Grossman Publishers, 1976
originally published as
La vida breve
Editorial Sudamericana, 1950

One of his compatriots, Carlos Maggi,
characterized Juan Carlos Onetti as "passionately
dispassionate, believing that he does not believe
in anything and only has faith in the lack of faith. There are
very few things that matter to him
—perhaps pure purity with the guarantee of its impossibility—
and nonetheless he keeps a vigil for
all things."

In the fluidity of Onetti's Protean world,
apparent contradictions
yield to the confluence of
unity
—or unities—and the "brief life"
or series of "brief lives"
link up to form an organic chain which is
simultaneously singular and multiple,
as in the opening pages of
A Brief Life where the mythopoeic hero,
Brausen,
holds up a vial of morphine in one hand
and a fountain pen in the other.

Brausen, the hero and creator;
Onetti, the author, and we, the readers of the writer's works,
will henceforth move within
the mythical geography of this world
born by metaphor
from many a "brief life."
For Santa María, the mythical locale of A Brief Life
becomes the locus of Onetti's subsequent works.

Djelal Kadir
Guest Editor

Chronology

Compiled by
DJELAL KADIR

1909. Juan Carlos Onetti is born on July 1 in Montevideo, the second of three sons born to Carlos Onetti and Honoria Borges de Onetti. Because Onetti is hesitant to talk about his childhood, detailed information on the author's early years is lacking. We do know, however, that he is the son of a customs official who moved his family frequently within Montevideo and that in Onetti's memory his was "a very happy family." A poor student, the author dropped out of secondary school and, having left his home as well, began a bohemian existence working at a number of odd jobs, including those of porter, waiter, ticket taker and wheat sifter.

1930. Onetti marries his cousin, María Amalia Onetti, and travels with her to Buenos Aires for the first time. In the Argentine capital, his first job is that of selling adding machines.

1932. Onetti writes the original version of *El pozo*, his first novel. The manuscript of this short work is lost.

1933. Onetti publishes his first short story, *"Avenida de Mayo—Diagonal—Avenida de Mayo"* in *La Prensa* of Buenos Aires. It is selected as one of the best ten stories in a contest sponsored by the newspaper. The manuscript of *Tiempo de abrazar*, a novel, circulates among his friends. The Argentine novelist Roberto Arlt recommends its publication.

DJELAL KADIR, Chairman for Spanish and Portuguese at Purdue University, has recently completed the first critical study of Onetti in English.

1934. Returns to Montevideo. He marries for the second time: María Julia Onetti, sister of his first wife.

1935. A second story, *"El obstáculo,"* appears in the daily *La Nación* (Buenos Aires), then under the editorship of the Argentine writer Eduardo Mallea.

1936. Onetti writes *"Los niños en el bosque,"* a long short story which was most likely intended to have been a novel. It does not appear in print until 1974. In September *"El posible Baldi,"* a short story, appears in *La Nación*. Without success Onetti attempts to travel to Spain as a volunteer in the Spanish Civil War.

1939. After initially working as the secretary to the editor of *Marcha*, Onetti is named editor-in-chief of the newly founded weekly published in Montevideo. *El pozo*, a reconstructed version of his first novel, is published in December in a limited edition of five hundred copies. Along with *Tierra de nadie* and *Para esta noche*, *El pozo* marks the first phase of Onetti's career as an innovator within the novelistic tradition of documenting the sordid, nightmarish realities of city life. Around this time, Onetti frequents the Café Metro, a gathering place for young intellectuals. His experiences there prove influential on his characterization of the lost generation of intellectuals in his subsequent works, especially in *Tierra de nadie*.

1940. Publishes *"Convalecencia"* in *Marcha* under the pseudonym of H. C. Ramos. The manuscript of his first novel, *Tiempo de abrazar*, is a finalist in a contest sponsored by Rinehart and Farrar of New York. It comes in second to the Peruvian Ciro Alegría's *El mundo es ancho y ajeno*. The original manuscript is lost except for various fragments which appear in *Marcha* in 1943.

1941. Onetti is employed as editor by the Reuters news agency in Montevideo. Moves back to Buenos Aires, where he resumes working for the same agency and later becomes editor of various periodicals. He remains in Buenos Aires until 1955. His novel *Tierra de nadie* is published by Losada and is awarded the second prize in the contest sponsored by the same publisher. The short story, *"Un sueño realizado"* appears in *La Nación*.

1943. Publication of *Para esta noche*. Onetti dedicates his novel to Eduardo Mallea. *"Mascarada,"* a short story, appears in *Apex* of Montevideo.

1944. Publishes *"La larga historia"* and *"Bienvenido, Bob"* (short stories). The latter is translated by Hanna Edwards and appears in *Odyssey Review*, Vol. 3, Number 2 (June, 1963), 192-199.

1945. Onetti marries for the third time: Elizabeth María Pekelharing.

1946. Publishes *"Regreso al sur"* and *"Esbjerg, en la costa"* both in *La Nación*. With his wife he translates Phoebe Atwood Taylor's *The Cape Cod Mystery*.

1949. Publishes *"La casa en la arena"* in *La Nación*. Díaz Grey, Onetti's most ubiquitous character and the "reader's friend" in subsequent works, appears for the first time as a protagonist in this story. We witness his genesis in the novel which is published the following year.

1950. Publication of *La vida breve* with which Onetti's fictional cosmos moves to the enchanted geography of the mythical, sometimes allegorical Santa María, an urban, Latin American equivalent of Faulkner's Yoknapatawpha County. The novel is a turning point in Onetti's career, initiating a series of books located in this imaginary terrain.

1951. Publishes the collection *Un sueño realizado y otros cuentos*. His daughter, Isabel María (Litti) is born.

1953. Publishes the novel *Los adioses*. Although Onetti purports not to understand Henry James, the problems of narrative point of view implied by the structure of the

work belie his modest claims. *"El álbum,"* a short story, appears in *Sur* of Buenos Aires.

1954-55. Back in Montevideo, Onetti translates Erskine Caldwell's *This Very Earth*. He works for a publicity firm and later for the periodical *Acción*. Marries for the fourth time: Dorotea (Dolly) Muhr, his present wife.

1956. Publishes the short story, *"Historia del Caballero de la Rosa y de la Virgen encinta que vino de Liliput."* Translates Paul Wellman's *The Comancheros*. Travels to Bolivia.

1957. Onetti is appointed Director of Municipal Libraries in Montevideo and is named to the board of directors of the Comedia Nacional. Publishes *"El infierno tan temido,"* a short story. Translates Burgess Drake's *Children of the Wind*.

1959. Publishes *Una tumba sin nombre*, a nouvelle. In a subsequent re-edition of this work, the title is changed to *Para una tumba sin nombre*, 3rd edition, 1968.

1960. Publishes *La cara de la desgracia*, short novel based on a six page short story, *"La larga historia,"* which first appears in 1944 in Montevideo.

1961. *El astillero*, considered by many as Onetti's major novel, is selected by the jury of a literary contest sponsored by Compañía General Fabril Editora and the novel is published by the company. His short story *"Jacob y el otro"* appears in a collection edited by Doubleday and Company of New York, *Ceremonia secreta y otros cuentos de América Latina*.

1962. Awarded the *Premio Nacional de Literatura*, Uruguay's national literary prize, for work published in 1959-60. Publishes *El infierno tan temido* (collection of short stories).

1963. The William Faulkner Foundation compiles a list of Spanish American novels not yet translated to English which are worthy of note. *El astillero* is singled out for Uruguay and is awarded "The William Faulkner Foundation Certificate of Merit for a Notable Novel to Juan Carlos Onetti for the distinguished book *El astillero*, Ibero-American Novel Award." *Tan triste como ella* (nouvelle) is published.

1964. Publishes "*Justo el treinta y uno*" (short story) in *Marcha*. Publication of *Juntacadáveres*, a sequel to *El astillero* whose events occur prior to those of the earlier novel.

1966. Onetti travels to New York to attend a meeting of P.E.N. Club.

1967. *Juntacadáveres* is a runner-up in the prestigious "Rómulo Gallegos" Prize which selects the best Spanish-American novel every five years. The Prize is awarded to the Peruvian Mario Vargas Llosa's *La casa verde*. A translation of *El astillero* appears in France.

1968. Onetti publishes "*La novia robada*" in *Papeles* of Caracas. It becomes the title story of *La novia robada y otros cuentos* published the same year. The English translation of *El astillero* (*The Shipyard,* translated by Rachel Caffyn) appears.

1969. Onetti travels to Chile to participate in a continental meeting of Latin American writers.

1970. Publication of his complete works, *Obras completas*, with an introduction by Emir Rodríguez Monegal, Mexico. Italian translation of *Juntacadáveres*. Italian translation of *La vida breve*. French translation of *Juntacadáveres*.

1971. Unsuccessful nominee for "Gran Premio de Literatura" (Uruguay). French translation of *La vida breve*. Onetti writes a prologue for the Italian edition of Roberto Arlt's *Los siete locos*.

1972. Italian translation of *El astillero*. Filming of *El astillero* begins in Mexico. In a survey by *Marcha* of thirty-five national writers, Onetti emerges as the best Uruguayan writer of the last fifty years.

1973. Publishes *La muerte y la niña* (novel). Onetti travels to Spain at the invitation of the Instituto de Cultura Hispánica to speak in a lecture series on Spanish American Literature sponsored by the Institute. It is Onetti's first public lecture.

1974. Publication of *Tiempo de abrazar* upon recovery of a greater part of the manuscript which had been misplaced since 1940. Included in the edition are almost all the short stories written between 1933 and 1955 and never collected into a volume or into the "Complete Works." January: Onetti forms part of the jury in a literary contest sponsored by *Marcha* to award the prize for the year's best short story. Onetti's reservations with respect to gratuitous elements of violence notwithstanding, the prize is awarded to a story deemed pornographic by the government authorities. Two members of the three-person jury are imprisoned. (The third was in Mexico at the time.) The editor of *Marcha* and the story's author are incarcerated and the weekly publication is shut down as well. Owing to the international outcry from the world's intellectuals and to the author's poor health, Onetti is finally released by the military authorities in May.

1975. As the social, political, and intellectual life in Uruguay worsens, so does Onetti's physical condition. Finally Onetti resigns his post as Director of Municipal Libraries because the authorities refuse his request for a leave to travel to Italy in order to accept a prize awarded to *El astillero* as the best work translated into Italian. Onetti leaves for Europe and remains there as the guest of the Instituto de Cultura Hispánica in Madrid. Onetti says that he is working on a big novel and a short story which he claims to be his last because of age, drunkenness and boredom. In the meantime, a collection of articles and short essays is expected to appear this year under the title of *Requiem por Faulkner y otros escritos*.

Liberation through Creation

EMIR RODRIGUEZ MONEGAL
Translated by Gregory Kolovakos

In 1939, Eladio Linacero, the protagonist of *El pozo* (The Pit) wrote that "the curious thing is that I'd be annoyed if someone were to say of me that I'm 'a dreamer.' It's absurd. I've lived like anyone else. If I want to talk about dreams today, it's not because I don't have anything else to say. It's because I simply feel like it. And if I choose the dream about the log cabin, it's not because I have any particular reason. There are other adventures which are more complete, more interesting, better ordered. But I'll stick with the cabin because it'll force me to recount a prologue, something that happened years ago in the real world. It might also be a plan to recount an 'event' and a dream." The plan referred to by Linacero developed not only into the ninety-nine pages of *El pozo* (a novel signed by J. C. Onetti) but also, ten years later, into a major work, *A Brief Life* (this time by Juan Carlos Onetti). In those ten years, the linear art of the first narrator matured into the complex structure of lives and dreams which are gathered up into a lengthy narrative by Juan María Brausen, Linacero's legitimate heir and another mask or *persona* of the author himself.

With economy Onetti confronts, from the first pages of *A Brief Life*, the two worlds in which the protagonist will move:

" 'Crazy world,' the woman said once, as if quoting, as if she were translating."

"I heard her through the wall. I imagined her mouth moving in front of the refrigerator's cold and vegetable odors as she faced the curtain of brown slats that hung rigidly between the afternoon sun and the bedroom, obscuring the disorder of the recently arrived furniture. I listened, absent-minded, without thinking about what she was saying."

The voice annoys Brausen but also tempts him. He feels attracted to it. The two worlds separated by the thin, promiscuous apartment wall will never be completely fused. In order to move from one to the other, Juan María Brausen will have to assume a new name; to cease to be Brausen and to begin to be "Juan María Arce." At a certain moment both worlds become tangential but they are never superimposed; they exist on different levels of reality; different laws govern them, and the game of living does not follow the same rules in both.

The world of Juan María Brausen is the world of responsibility and routine, of boredom, of the misunderstanding that we call love. There is a moment in the novel in which the protagonist attempts to define himself:

"Meanwhile I'm this small, timid man, unchanging, married to the only woman whom I ever seduced or who ever seduced me, not only incapable of being otherwise, but of possessing the will power to be otherwise. A little man despised to the degree of pity he inspires, a little man confused amid a legion of little men to whom the heavenly kingdom was promised. Ascetic, as Stein says, because of my incapacity for passion and not because of the absurd belief in a conviction that in time becomes mutilated. This person, me in the taxicab, nonexistent, a mere incarnation of the idea of a Juan María Brausen, the biped symbol of a cheap puritanism, made up of refusals—no to alcohol, no to tobacco, an equivalent no to women—not anyone, in reality; . . ."

While Brausen's existence becomes degraded until it touches bottom, the world on the other side of the fragile wall begins to exercise its fascination over him. At first its meaning seems obvious: it is an escape, a flight from routine. But it is also real (as Brausen will come to discover) and it even imposes its own rules. One day Brausen avails himself of the absence of his neighbor, La Queca, and visits the empty apartment. From that moment Brausen begins to conceive his revenge. Not in his own rat-like existence, but in the next-door world. Upon entering that world it is as if all his moral values (those values in which he can no longer believe) would be inverted: he, the man of only one woman, will be able to become a pimp; he, always fearful of making Gertrudis, his legitimate wife, aware of the imperfection of her breasts (she had had a mastectomy), will want to avenge "all the wrongs that I could possibly remember" by the premeditated murder of La Queca.

A harsh confrontation marks Brausen's entrance into the next-door world. In his first attempt to make contact with La Queca, Brausen (vacillating, improvising) is kicked out by Ernesto, one of La Queca's lovers. While he is picking himself up and brushing off his clothes, soiled at last, Brausen understands that he has been accepted, that now he is beginning to be Juan María Arce. Violence seems to be the rule of this other side's game. But it is not the only rule. Little by little, Arce discovers the true meaning of this world, euphorically anticipated in his visit to the empty apartment. It is a world, like that of Lewis Carroll in *Through the Looking Glass*, in which

images (values) are inverted. In a second visit, when the aggressive Ernesto is away, Brausen makes up with La Queca.

With her, the routine of sex is converted into something else: "If I forgot her (he thinks while he watches her walking through the room), I could desire her, make her stay and infect me with her silent happiness, press my body against hers and afterward leap out of bed to feel and look at myself naked, harmonious, shining like a young Greek god, from the youth transmitted through skin and mucus, overflowing with my third-hand vigor." From these experiences of Brausen's, a new man, not just a new name, is created. When he agrees to go to Montevideo with La Queca on a trip financed by an old lover of hers, the new experience of degradation allows him to look at himself from the illusory distance of Brausen and to feel "irresponsible for what he (Arce) might think and do"; he sees himself "slowly descending into total cynicism, into an invincible depth of vileness from which (Arce) would be forced to raise himself in order to become me."

In order to be able to assume completely this world of the other truth (the world of Arce), Brausen has to purify himself by killing La Queca; a few minutes then would be sufficient to relieve himself of all that can be said, "to be left empty of all that I've had to swallow since my adolescence, of all the words drowned by laziness, by lack of faith, by the feeling of the uselessness of talking." When Brausen-Arce arrives at the apartment to kill La Queca he discovers that she has just been murdered by Ernesto. The reality of violence in the next-door world overwhelms him.

Because Brausen never ceased being Brausen. Not even when he frees himself of his commitments (his job, his wife, his friendships); not even when he buries, with Raquel, the nostalgia of his youth in Montevideo; not even when he lives for so many months as Arce. He then rejects the rules of the bourgeois game which he was living, he changes his outlook, but, profoundly, he remains Brausen. His reaction to the murder of La Queca proves it. In the presence of the brutal reality, Arce disappears—the new game (*his* game now) demanded that he in turn kill Ernesto. Instead, it is a renewed Brausen who decides to protect the murderer, who attempts to save him, creating a new life for him. Perhaps Brausen already feels that Ernesto has killed for him, although only later does he come to formulate this thought, to feel that he is responsible: "He's no more than a part of me: he and all the others have lost their individuality, they're parts of me." In their desperate attempt at escape, Brausen and Ernesto arrive in Santa María and end up being arrested there. Paradoxically, the prison restores freedom to Brausen: "This was what I was searching for from the beginning, since the death of the man who lived with Gertrudis for five years; to be free, to be irresponsible in regard to others, to conquer effortlessly for myself a true solitude." Meanwhile, his escape has introduced him into a new dimension of reality, a third world which is farther from the next-door apartment and as ancient as the novel itself.

Before Brausen learned that it was possible to enter La Queca's world which ran chaotically parallel to his own, the need to escape routine had forced him to invent an imaginary world. The first image of that world which comes to him is that of Díaz Grey, a doctor in his forties who practices in Santa María, a sleepy town by the River Plate. While Brausen hides from himself in Buenos Aires and gradually is metamorphosed into Arce, the story of Díaz Grey is slowly growing in his imagination as another means of escape. The world in which Díaz Grey lives is a transparent stylization of the reality which oppresses Brausen, in the same way in which Santa María is built with fragments of Buenos Aires (which was baptized Santa María del Buen Aire by Pedro de Mendoza), of Montevideo, of Rosario, of Colonia do Sacramento: all cities located on the River Plate or its principal tributary, the Paraná.

To describe Brausen's third *persona*, Onetti abandons all pretense of realism. If in the presentation of the double life of Brausen-Arce one could find an echo of that story by Hawthorne, "Wakefield," in which

a man hides from his wife and goes to live under another name, close to her but invisible, Borges is the most evident model for this new avatar of Brausen. Although the surface of Onetti's story continues to abound in details of sordid, exasperated naturalism, the dimensions of time and space, the identities of his characters, are susceptible to alterations. A decision of the writer's will or a whim of his imagination can alter the surface of the narrative world and petrify its underlying moral values.

Just as Arce, at the end of his adventures with Ernesto, dissolves into Brausen—and the policeman who detains him as Ernesto's protector identifies him correctly: "You're the other. . . . You're Brausen"—, Díaz Grey in turn will have become the protagonist of the novel, his fictional reality having assimilated Brausen. The creature ends by absorbing the creator. Díaz Grey's world, invented by Brausen before the reader's eyes, ends by being the "real" narrative world of the novel, and the words "The End" on the last page prove that, in effect, the only "truth" in this novel (as in all novels, despite the pretenses of realism) is the truth of its text. It is only then that the fairness of this warning can be understood: " 'I felt that I was waking up,' says the protagonist, 'not from this dream but from another, incomparably longer, that included this one and in which I had dreamed I was dreaming this dream.' " Once again, as in Eladio Linacero's narrative, we have here both a story and a dream.

Another reading of *A Brief Life* also seems possible. Instead of considering the novel (as has been done until now) from the mimetic point of view, as a testimony concerning a world without moral values, the reader can follow Brausen only on his inner adventure. Then it is not just a question of escaping from reality, living a brief life or inventing a story to make into a film or to develop into a novel. It is a matter of creating another entire reality, of competing with the creator himself. Gradually, and almost without realizing it, Brausen frees the forces of his imagination. While he lives his life of gray routine, or the more exciting but also commonplace life of Arce, or the always retouchable life of Díaz Grey, Brausen explores the unlimited provinces of creation.

The whole novel, then, acquires depth in time and in space. Instead of developing three more or less novelesque stories that are juxtaposed but which happen in separated worlds governed by their own laws, the book sets its different anecdotes on the same spatial and temporal frame; that common territory of the three stories is the experience of narrative creation: the essential theme which links their separate but simultaneous existence. It is obvious that in *A Brief Life* Onetti has wanted to explore literary creation from two simultaneous and even inseparable points of view: the theoretical and the practical. His novel analyzes literary creation while he is creating it. Onetti certainly does not do this in the purely critical form which Cortázar will use in *Hopscotch* (1963) which reflected the influence of European writers such as André Gide (in the *Faux-monnayeurs* and the *Journal des Faux-monnayeurs*) or Aldous Huxley in *Point Counterpoint*. What Onetti does is to show his protagonist inventing first a double and then a parallel world into which he and his double will enter. From this decision comes the necessary distinction between an author (Onetti) and a narrator (Brausen) and a second distinction between the narrator and the other characters who are purely novelistic creatures. With this complex but fair device, Onetti attains a greater depth. He also succeeds in divesting the traditional theme of the double of all abstraction and intellectualism by approaching it from a passionately existential point of view.

Moreover, he manages to give a deeper content to the novel's obvious message. It is true that the liberation from routine and from the soul's devaluation occurs when we find the truth about ourselves, when we strip ourselves of inhibitions and compromises, when we dispel misunderstandings (Brausen's awakening from the dream after having purified himself through "Arce"); but that liberation may also occur through creation, through the forces which the creator unleashes when he remakes the

world, when he discovers with amazement his own power and the richness of life. Thus, the protagonist manages to uncover—in one of his many dreams—the true ambition of this writer, the final message of his work. He says "Sometimes I wrote and at other times imagined the adventures of Díaz Grey, approximated Santa María through the foliage of the square and the roofs of buildings near the river, wondered at the doctor's increasing tendency to wallow over and over again in the same event, at the need—which was infecting me—to suppress words and situations, to attain a single moment that might express it all: to Díaz Grey and to me, therefore to the entire world."

Brausen, in some symbolic way, has also been metamorphosed into his creator, into Juan Carlos Onetti. The character, the narrator and the author end by being one and by sharing the existential reality of this intense, strange, complex novel.

Read in 1950, *A Brief Life* seemed to be above all a bold experiment, a work unlike any other in the Latin American novel of that time in spite of the works already published by Borges, Arlt, Marechal, Agustín Yáñez, Carpentier and Miguel Angel Asturias. But read today, next to books such as *Hopscotch, One Hundred Years of Solitude, Three Trapped Tigers, A Change of Skin, Cobra,* or *Betrayed by Rita Hayworth,* Onetti's novel runs the risk of seeming too traditional. This is not the case, however. Because of its precision in establishing the boundaries between the various imaginary worlds, because of its subtle presentation and exploration of the problem of the double personality (a theme which *Hopscotch* would also take up), because of its own stylistic tension, *A Brief Life* is the most important forerunner of the new Latin American novel, the work from which nearly all the others (whether they know it or not) originate.

This article originally appeared as part of Emir Rodríguez Monegal's Prologue to Onetti's *Obras Completas* (Mexico: Aguilar, 1970).

The Novel as Self-Creation

HUGO J. VERANI

One of the richest and most complex novelistic expressions in Spanish-American fiction, *A Brief Life* is the culmination and synthesis of Onetti's narrative art. In this novel, the principle which gives artistic continuity to the rest of Onetti's narrative work is most evident; that is, the conception of literature as an undertaking of the imagination, as an act of inventing one's own verbal universe.

As is well known, this affirmation of faith in the creative powers of language is one of the innovations that distinguishes the contemporary Latin American novel. Octavio Paz, among others, points out that the most important works in contemporary Spanish-American literature are essentially imaginative works in which the writer attempts the invention or foundation of a world. In this connection Borges' pre-eminence is established, for one of the guiding principles of his short stories is the endless configuration of fictitious universes. But in *One Hundred Years of Solitude*, as in *Hopscotch* and in other novels where verbal exploration of reality is even more extreme (*A Change of Skin, The Obscene Bird of Night*), the authors also attempt to restore language to its original power of creation, to turn the novel into a basically literary experience. Marina Mizzau—following Edoardo Sanguinetti—refers to this narrative device, which consists of making the very act of creating a novel the object of narration, and distinguishes it as the convention that could give unity and meaning to the contemporary

novel in general. The reader of twentieth-century literature is confronted with a narrative in which several realities are superimposed upon one another so as to create what Mizzau has called "a reality that is continually belied as such and established as fiction."

This literary convention constitutes one of the distinctive traits of *A Brief Life*. The principal narrator, Brausen, introduces second and even third orders of reality that modify the initial conditions. The interweaving of the three contiguous stories—Brausen's life, his gradual evolution into Arce and into Díaz Grey—, the converging development and final fusion of the narrator's triple spatial and mental extension, reveal the prevalent structural principle of Onetti's literary creation. Brausen founds a world (Santa María); he imagines two other ways of life, and these two simultaneous experiences begin to acquire autonomy, become independent of their creator, and finally displace the fiction that gave them form. Ultimately, therefore, these worlds are reflected as one literary reality imposing itself upon another.

A novel in the making and a narrator in the process of creating his own reality are, understandably, a further source of complexity and difficulty of interpretation to the reader accustomed to traditional fiction. As if reflected in a set of facing mirrors, reality branches off into variations of the original story. The novel renews itself endlessly in exploratory reiterations. Each successive episode of *A Brief Life* introduces a variation of the same basic conflict, duplicates the preceding fiction in a perpetual symmetry that intensifies Brausen's helplessness

HUGO VERANI is Assistant Professor of Latin American literature at the University of California, Davis, and is completing a book on the narrative of Juan Carlos Onetti.

and nullifies every effort to shape his own destiny: "Nothing is interrupted, nothing ends; although the shortsighted might get lost in changes of circumstance and character."

The novel becomes a stage and each character, time and again, plays a part, participates in an absurd, never-ending game—the game of life: "I kiss his feet, I applaud the courage of he who accepts each and every one of the laws of a game he did not invent and was not asked if he wanted to play." The play-conception of life, the poetics of fiction-within-fiction, and the progressive disintegration of Brausen's personality are the coordinates that give unity to all the narrative sequences of *A Brief Life*. Brausen is aware of his inability to function, to become a part of the world. By means of his interior duplication and his use of masks (it is no coincidence that the ending of the novel takes place on the final day of carnival season), Brausen imposes upon himself an end that alters his passive and routine existence. The act of creation becomes the only reason for being, the mechanism that justifies his entire existence.

A Brief Life is also an example of what has been called a "novel-within-a-novel." The original fiction serves as the initial phase for the creation of another world— a completely relative world that exists only in the mind of the narrator-protagonist. The ambiguity in *A Brief Life* results from the confrontation of the reality created by the author, and the reality created by the narrator's imagination. The fictitious setting of Santa María as well as the characters begin to free themselves from Brausen's influence, displacing him as the generator of fiction.

As Leon Livingstone has studied in a broader context, the technique of fiction-within-fiction and the interior duplication of characters become a symbolic statement. By doubting the validity of the distinction between the real and the fictional in a universe whose component parts are interchangeable, a disconcerting perplexity is created in the mind of the reader. "What is involved is not merely a question of escapism, of idealization or the romantic or mystical flights from reality, but of the reinter-pretation of reality to exclude mutually hostile opposites by making microcosm and macrocosm reciprocal facets of a total reality. It is the world of absolute relativity in which the subject not only perceives objective reality but creates it; a world in which imagination creates reality, in which fiction becomes truth."[1]

A Brief Life reflects a conception of existence as a network of brief episodes or stages. For Brausen, life is a series of "little suicides," of "deaths and resurrections," a world in which the transitory quality of life precludes any attempt at human communication, or any possibility of establishing an affective bond. For him, then, invention is the only way to self-realization, the only chance to give meaning to his life or to justify his existence: "But I had the entire night, this Saturday night, to save myself. I would be saved if I began to write the screenplay for Stein, if I finished two pages, or at least one, if I captured the woman who would enter Díaz Grey's office and conceal herself behind the folding screen; if perhaps I wrote only a single sentence." Brausen's need to invent his own world, to impose his own concept of reality, is the essential theme of *A Brief Life*. It is also one of the most significant tendencies of the contemporary novel. In the words of Robbe-Grillet: "What constitutes the novelist's strength is precisely that he invents, that he invents quite freely, without a model. The remarkable thing about modern fiction is that it asserts this characteristic quite deliberately, to such a degree that invention and imagination become, at the limit, the very subject of the book."

The world appears as a continuous invention of possible existences, which, once accepted, must be continued until exhausted, until the end of the imagined life is reached and a new variation begins, a new brief life. The characters are aware that they are playing a part and, having accepted the convention, they are obliged to live by its rules. This is one the essential tenets of Onetti's narrative: that life is a farce, a lie, a never-ending game. This is an idea that is sketched by Onetti in his early short stories and which, some thirty years later, emerges as the guiding motif of *The Ship-yard* (1961).

Any attempt by Brausen to free himself from his own inhibitions and to find a new reason for living is condemned to fail. Nevertheless, he finds a way of avoiding the meaningless nature of his life, and this way is the creative adventure. To elude nothingness, he relies upon his imagination; he becomes Díaz Grey, the protagonist of the film script that he is writing, and he becomes Arce, the name he assumes as the lover of the prostitute, La Queca. Brausen knows he will survive only if he maintains the illusion of pretending to be Arce in La Queca's apartment, and if he continues to be Díaz Grey in Santa María: "Meanwhile, I was almost not working and scarcely existing; I was Arce at the regular drunken parties with La Queca, in the growing pleasure of beating her, amazed that it was easy and necessary to do it; I was Díaz Grey, writing or thinking about him, astonished by life's richness and my power." Brausen's behavior is characterized by this intrinsic inability to adapt to life. Brausen, insignificant and frustrated as an individual, acquires new powers over his own actions in the movie script and in La Queca's apartment. The masks that he puts on provide a means of transcending his existence and yield a fresh vital essence, a new hope for continuity.

Brausen imagines the character of Dr. Díaz Grey as a possibility for vital enrichment of his own life. At first, there is no ambiguity in the relationship between the narrator and the character invented by him. With the displacement of the point of view from first to third person during the process of the doctor's early characterization (the first-person identifies Brausen), the two characters are clearly differentiated and Díaz Grey's subordination to Brausen is maintained. At the same time a gradual process of affirmation of the dream as an absolute verbal reality takes place. Díaz Grey begins to acquire autonomy in Brausen's mind; he establishes ties, avails himself of his own fantasies, and creates his own world without depending upon the man who invented him. Díaz Grey then be-

gins to intuit the existence of his creator, a superior being who directs his movements; and the disturbing possibility of inverting the existential relationship between them is implied. Díaz Grey feels he is an "incomprehensible and insignificant manifestation of life, caprice engendered by caprice, the timid inventor of Brausen." He discovers that he, too, is playing a part and, like any being which considers itself real, the doctor seeks to decipher the mystery of his creation, in this case, by confronting Brausen, a deity indifferent to his own creation ("He was calling my name in vain"). The cyclical configuration of existence is repeated once more: the boundaries between the dreamer and the dreamed one are blurred and the reader senses still another interior duplication. The narrative discourse is uniform, a condition which is maintained until the last chapter at which point the relationship is inverted. Díaz Grey becomes an independent first-person narrator using the present tense, and Brausen vanishes from the text. More importantly, it raises another question: that of the continuity of consciousness. "Universal history is the history of a single man," says Borges in *Historia de la Eternidad*. The notion of the progressive dissolution of individual personality, a key aspect of Borges' short stories, is also a predominant motif of *A Brief Life*.

At the same time that Díaz Grey begins to suspect that he is a figment of someone's imagination and seeks to assert his independence, we witness the birth of another character, Arce. Lying motionless, Brausen imagines from "this side"[2] of the wall, the movements and activities in La Queca's apartment. He enters her apartment and a new atmosphere that impels him to "shake the past from my shoulders, the memory of all that could serve to identify me"; the start of a new "brief life" is suggested. Brausen pretends to be someone else in order to become part of another world and to generate a further transformation of his being: a new name, a new perspective, a new character that must gradually be delineated. If passivity and frustration are inherent in Brausen, Arce will represent just the opposite; his life will be guided and conditioned by passion, even by sadistic brutality. His evolution into his new role is, in a sense, systematic. He imposes upon himself new rules of conduct, and gradually adopts a new personality in an alien world of ruffians and prostitutes.

The inexhaustible game of creation persists throughout the novel and culminates in self-creation. Brausen projects the image of his creator, and through the emergence of the latter as a character in his own novel, we perceive the root of all existence as an act of spiritual creation, an act of love. Brausen himself gave life to other characters and satisfied his creative urge by incorporating his own creator into the fiction. It is a way of declaring his freedom and of affirming the "real" existence of his imagined world, of postulating the independent destiny of his own creative effort.

Brausen's two imaginary projections of himself superimpose themselves upon one another simultaneously—in time as well as in space, and finally, in the last two chapters, by removing the principal narrator and shaping another order of reality. But the parallel in the temporal development of the stories is not merely a literary artifice; it reaches more profound dimensions. The characters in all the stories are projections of the original triad: Brausen, Gertrudis, and Stein. These projections, which are direct at the beginning, gradually obtain autonomy and become independent of their creator. The constellation of three characters remains unaltered, and each new scene repeats the same basic, past situations. In his unceasing attempt to transcend immediate reality and his own limitations, Brausen discovers a multiple world that repeats his image perpetually, accumulating a series of brief lives, an infinite number of possibilities, reinforced by the open form of the novel, and leaving the reader with an unmistakable impression of hopelessness.

A Brief Life has no narrative thread, in the traditional sense of the term; instead, it introduces a series of cyclical mutations of a single image. Onetti does not emphasize the mimetic quality of narrative. The aim of his fiction is not to reflect an existent real-ity, a factual order, but, on the contrary, to create an essentially fabulated reality invested with mythic significance.

The final two chapters place parallel scenes in a contrapuntal relationship with each other and, in the process, suspend reality. Both chapters remain inconclusive. Onetti himself affirms that *A Brief Life* is "an open book" and, certainly, this novel is a forerunner of *Hopscotch* and *Three Trapped Tigers*—the two most representative open novels in Spanish-American literature—and shares with them the tendency toward openness that proliferates in contemporary literature. Thematic tensions are left unresolved, since a definite anecdotal resolution is not forthcoming, and internal relationships remain potent, open to new stimuli.

In the final episodes of *A Brief Life,* a subtle scheme of correspondences is established. Brausen's escape with Ernesto unfolds in an analogous manner to that of Díaz Grey with Lagos, Oscar Owen, and the violinist. La Queca (murdered by Ernesto) and Elena Sala have died and their deaths are described in almost the same way, with minor linguistic variations. Díaz Grey and his group are also fugitives from justice, because Owen murdered a policeman; Ernesto is a reflection of the adventurer Owen. Brausen flees Buenos Aires and heads for Santa María (from "reality" to "fiction"); Díaz Grey retreats in the opposite direction, from Santa María to Buenos

Aires. Both have erased their past and can finally "live without memory or foresight": Brausen (as Arce) in the timeless present of Santa María, the town he invented, where he seeks refuge and a freer self, unaffected by his past. Díaz Grey, exalted by the illusory liberation, continues to indulge his fantasies of amorous conquests, this time with the violinist, the last female character in the novel. Both men come to the same end, with no possible means of escape; but they are now free of consequences, relieved of the need to attribute meaning to life: "Without running from anyone, without wanting to meet anyone, dragging our feet a little, more due to happiness than fatigue."

As the meanings unfold, the depth of their implications is revealed. Brausen's search (as Arce), his victory in solitude as an end in himself, free of responsibility, ends when the policeman arrests him, saying: "You're the other. . . . You're Brausen." Three narratives interweave and merge into one. The first is the fantasy in Brausen's mind (his imagined freedom from responsibilities). Next is the "real," Brausen's arrest (as Brausen, not as Arce), revealing the cyclical nature of existence and the futility of trying to alter one's personal destiny. The third, which affirms the powers of fiction, becomes explicit here and is further strengthened in the following, ultimate chapter.

Artistic creation acquires the same degree of reality as the original story; it develops its own rules. Brausen enters into the world that he himself has invented, where, "they were all mine, born from me, and I felt pity and love for them. . . . The hotel was on the corner of the square, and the construction of the block of houses coincided with my memories and with the changes I had imposed while imagining the doctor's story." But the novel attains its full significance as an affirmation of the powers of fiction in a scene rich in unsuspected implications, a scene depicting the end of Brausen's trip to Santa María superimposed upon the end of a novel published fourteen years later: the expulsion of Larsen (Junta) in *Juntacadáveres* [Corpse-gatherer]. On entering a restaurant in Santa María, Brausen finds a group of people he does not recognize. He becomes the indifferent spectator of a scene, which, as James E. Irby has observed, is "with small variations, the same scene in which Larsen and his prostitutes are driven out of Santa María, that is to say, the ending of another story, filled with understatements that in themselves presuppose still another series of events and another time. Brausen shows no sign of recognizing anyone present, among whom there is one, referred to as 'Doctor' by his companions, who is none other than Díaz Grey, as is revealed in *Juntacadáveres*."[3]

Since Brausen does not recognize the inhabitants of Santa María gathered in the restaurant of the Hotel Berna (Díaz Grey, Larsen, María Bonita, Jorge Malabia, and Lanza), the control that he thinks he had over his creation disappears. The literary universe that he had peopled frees itself entirely from his influence. It is in this literary freedom that Brausen-Onetti finds spiritual fulfillment.

Brausen does not appear at all in the last chapter. Díaz Grey has gradually acquired his own individuality and supplants Brausen as narrator. He expresses himself in the first-person and in the present indicative. Up to this point in the novel, the past-tense had been used; with the present, however, the narrator is esthetically closer to the reader and the latter's distance from the story is minimized. Even more important is the illusion of timelessness which is achieved by halting the time flow of the narration.

One cycle is closed and another is begun in this chapter. Lagos invents Mr. Albano, a new imaginary projection, as a telephone code for keeping up with the progress of the police pursuit; but the "interest . . . in the impossible appearance of Mr. Albano" increases, and Díaz Grey begins to imagine future encounters. Isolated from the world in an eternal and empty present, the survivors of Brausen's dream await the inception of a new illusion with a new game, in order to conceal their abandonment, and to protect their world from total disintegration. Reality is reflected and subdivided endlessly.

The ending of the novel coincides with the last day of the carnival season, and the relationship between carnivalesque make-believe and existence itself is disconcerting. To avoid detection by the police, Díaz Grey and his companions roam the streets in costumes. Salvation depends on choosing the appropriate disguise: "Suddenly I imagine that everything—escape, salvation, the future that joins us and that only I can remember—relies on our not making a mistake in choosing the costumes." Life appears transformed into a mascarade, but behind each mask or costume there are only the various transformations of the self, the dissolution of the self into a plurality of masks, the representation of one role after another.

Each of Brausen's transformations is to be understood as a possible course of living —different circumstances, different names, but always subject to existential cyclies in which the same being is repeated: "I'm the only man on earth, I'm the measure," exclaims Brausen in a direct echo of Borges' phrase: "Universal history is that of a single man." Toward the end of the novel, referring to the violinist, Lagos reaffirms the multiplicity of the self, the diverse roles that man must play in life and, at the same time synthesizes the meaning of the work: "It's Elena. Nothing is interrupted, nothing ends; although the shortsighted might get lost in changes of circumstance and character. But not you, doctor. Listen: that trip you made with Elena pursuing Oscar, isn't it exactly the same trip that they're taking this dawn in a launch from Tigre—a ballerina, a bull-

fighter, a guardsman, a king?"

The conclusion of the novel symbolizes another cyclical return to the beginning. Díaz Grey leaves with the violinist, having no certain destination in mind. But now the virginal violinist *is* in fact Elena, who had previously represented Gertrudis, just as she [Gertrudis] was reborn in Raquel, her younger sister, the fifteen-year-old girl before the fall. In the fiction, the violinist is perpetuated, pure and immaculate, in a timeless present.

Onetti's narrative art is a response to the necessity of justifying existence, of overcoming the limitations of the human condition. Far from being a gratuitous esthetic game, his work draws its only narrative material from the empirical world and, above all, from subjective experiences. But, the narrative universe of Onetti—and *A Brief Life* is probably his most representative novel—arises as a fictitious entity distinguished by the projection of his own inner search to the sphere of the imaginary, to the sphere of pure invention. "A novel should be integral," says Onetti, and the dominant aspect of his work is, indeed, the masterly integration of narrative strata— the intimate fusion of content and form—a synthesis that is essential to all art, because it conjoins the inquiry into man's destiny ("I only want to express man's adventure, the senselessness of life"), and the need to create that dominates Onetti's entire work: "I believe that literature is art, a sacred thing. Accordingly, never a means but always an end in itself." ◯

1. Leon Livingstone, "Interior Duplication and the Problem of Form in the Modern Spanish Novel," *PMLA*, 4 (1958), p. 394.
2. Alain Robbe-Grillet, *For a New Novel* (N.Y.: Grove Press, 1965), p. 32.
3. James E. Irby, *"Aspectos formales de La vida breve de J. C. Onetti,"* in *Actas del Tercer Congreso Internacional de Hispanistas* (Mexico: El Colegio de Mexico, 1970), p. 458.

A longer version of this article was published as *"Teoría v creación de la novela: La vida breve,"* in *Cuadernos Hispanoamericanos*, N⁰ 292-294 (1974), pp. 433-464. The present version was translated from the Spanish by the author.

Dream and Spatial Form

JOHN DEREDITA

Linear narration plays its part in the over-all development of *A Brief Life* since the basic narrator, Brausen, tells his retrospective story in a generally diachronic succession. For example, the titles of several chapters identify key moments of the symbolic spring, summer and fall that lead Brausen from the dissolution of his marriage through the death of the prostitute La Queca, and these titles underscore temporal indications in the text. Brausen further marks transitions in his schizoid trajectory as Juan María Brausen (his public role as husband and adman) and Juan María Arce (his impersonation as La Queca's kept man) according to the shift of seasons or periods while he watches time pass and waits for events to fill his void. The fiction-within-fiction of Díaz Grey (the role projected by Brausen in the film scenario that is the second of his short lives) also has a predominantly linear order from its first episode (the appearance of the enigmatic Elena Sala in his office) to the carnival sequence of the last chapter where Díaz Grey seems to be embarking on a romance with the violinist, the adolescent virgin of his (and Brausen's) dreams. Besides lending clarity to the several narrative tracks, this linear axis of the narrative supports the existential theme of personal disintegration in time.

The defining gesture of *A Brief Life*, however, is posed against diachrony. The novel exhaustively tests the power of fantasy and fictional imagination as a counter to the flow of time, which is intolerable for the Onettian subjectivity. Fantasy, as Freud suggested in "The Relation of the Poet to Daydreaming," amalgamates several dimensions of time.

One may say that a fantasy at one and the same time hovers between three periods of time. . . . The activity of fantasy in the mind is linked up with some current impression, occasioned by some event in the present, which had the power to rouse an intense desire. From there, it wanders back to the memory of an early experience, generally belonging to infancy, in which this wish was fulfilled. Then it creates for itself a situation which is to emerge in the future, representing the fulfillment of the wish—this is the daydream of fantasy, which now carries in it traces both of the occasion which engendered it and of some past memory.[1]

Fantasy postulates a temporally imprecise situation "which is to emerge in the future." Early in Part I, in the key chapter entitled "Salvation," Brausen describes the imaginative genesis of Dr. Díaz Grey in terms that parallel Freud's model. The first scene in the Doctor's office—the scene in which Díaz Grey is introduced —is built on Brausen's first encounter with the young Gertrudis in Montevideo (when, in the Onettian pattern observed by James Irby, she seduced *him*). That meeting initiated the love that has definitively

JOHN DEREDITA teaches Spanish American literature at Bryn Mawr College.

died with her emblematic disfigurement in the medical operation performed just prior to the time of the first chapter. In the "Salvation" chapter, in the presence of an adolescent portrait reminding him of the Gertrudis he loved, Brausen recalls their first meeting and then observes that at some point in the present, the eve of Gertrudis' return from the first of several visits home to Mother in this period of break-up, Gertrudis would have to spring out of the portrait to wait her turn in Díaz Grey's office. This "Gertrudis-Elena Sala" would go smiling into the waiting room, the same woman that Brausen met as Gertrudis some years ago in Montevideo. The particular moment of love's awakening is what Brausen seeks to posit in his fantasy. "I knew then [in Montevideo] that I wanted to be resurrected now with the name of Díaz Grey." Like Freud's subject, Brausen's consciousness on the verge of launching his necessary fiction sustains three moments of time: the present with its sense of deprivation; the past moment of fulfillment with the young Gertrudis; the indefinite future of the fiction. The narration, of course, departs from simple linearity by combining the exposition of the Montevideo scene with the episode of consciousness in Buenos Aires (which is in linear sequence with the preceding chapters) and the projected fictional episode in Díaz Grey's town of Santa María. Onetti's version of the origin of fantasy corresponds broadly to Freud's, except that the unconscious return to a gratifying moment of infancy is replaced by the conscious memory of erotic fulfillment with Gertrudis. Also, in Onetti, the fulfillment contained in the fantasy itself is mitigated, reduced from the sexual encounter of the Montevideo episode to the titillation Díaz Grey feels rather vaguely in Elena's presence. Díaz Grey is the creature of a (surrogate) fictional imagination rather than the product of a strictly escapist fantasy. As such he and his situation reproduce problematic features of the imaginer's existence. Nevertheless, Brausen is represented as believing he can regain past fulfillment by positing it in the new key of fiction.

The play of fantasy, then, works against the linear time of aging and of the subject's failed careers in bourgeois institutions: marriage and advertising. The operations of fantasy are present not only in the large structure of the novel but also in the specific details of the discourse. For example, critics have pointed out the remarkable frequency of the verbs "imagine," "invent," "imitate," "mimic," which become a code over and above the immediate context of their use, a code underscoring the thematics of dream, art and the transformation of personality.

The first chapter of the novel introduces the texture of imagination and can serve to illustrate it. An excellent example of the subjectivist focus of Onetti's fiction, the chapter consists exclusively of Brausen's recollection of the afternoon following Gertrudis' surgery, when he was alone in his apartment. His outward passivity and confinement are offset by his mental vagaries. Overhearing a conversation between his new neighbor (whom he will later know as La Queca), and her man-of-the-moment, he immediately sets about imagining the scene in the adjacent apartment. Another instance of imagining occurs as he reflects on Gertrudis' operation, conjecturing about the instant when the surgeon was using his scalpel, and imagining the scar in its present and future states as well as the new mummery of lovemaking that Gertrudis' deformity will require. A reference to the film scenario literally anticipates the sublimating function which *that* imaginative effort will perform, but the macabre metaphoric transformation his language works upon the detached breast already represents a sublimation through fantasy: "It was going to be impossible to write the film script Stein had spoken to me about while I could not manage to forget that cut breast, shapeless now, flattened out on the operating table like a jellyfish, offering itself like a wineglass." The poetic arabesques of Onetti's discourse subordinate outward incidents and determine a characteristically slow tempo. The episodic flow of many chapters is diverted as fantasies engender other fantasies. Brausen may imagine the daydream of another character, as when he begins to believe in La Queca's imagined demons, whom he suspects of coming between him and her; or, when within his literary projection, he conceives of Díaz Grey entertaining a fantasy of an idyl with a younger Elena Sala in Buenos Aires "in a past that was never going to happen" and, within the fantasy, having another daydream of escape in a purely oneiric decor, "I imagine," says Díaz Grey's monologue, "moving away from a small town made up of motels; from a silent village in which naked couples amble through small gardens." Counting the always implicit presence of Onetti as the initial dreamer in this unremittingly self-reflexive text, we arrive in the latter example at a fifth power of dream.

The title *A Brief Life* of course defines itself in relation to time. It connotes both mortality and the anti-temporal aspect of fantasy and art. The bordello scene where Miriam the madam, better known as Mami, sings "*La vie est brève*" is emblematic of both poles of the tension between disintegration and dream

> La vie est brève
> un peu d'amour
> un peu de rêve
> et puis bonjour.
> La vie est brève
> un peu d'espoir
> un peu de rêve
> et puis bonsoir.

The song breezily sums up the mortality of all things, including dreams. It is typical of the persistent irony of the novel that in his narration, Brausen sees Mami returning to youth and innocence as she performs the song, while one of the prostitutes remarks that she is killing herself. Brausen projects onto Mami the hope advanced by all the artists and dreamers of the novel: that they may conquer time. Opposition to time is also the subject of the other textual reference to the title, which comes when Brausen enters La Queca's empty apartment, making his first surreptitious move into her world: "I was calm and excited each time my feet touched the floor, believing that I was moving into the atmosphere of a brief life in which there was not enough time to become involved, to repent, or to age."

The title further refers to the way this novel (and novels in general) press time into the compass of a text, discontinuously from the temporal flow of the writer's and reader's existences. The critic Guido Castillo has remarked that the distinctive process of *A Brief Life* is the spatialization of time, the positing of a space where different moments "besides being successive are also, and above all, simultaneous, because all those moments are *at the same time* in the novel and not merely one after the other."[2] Castillo does not, however, discuss spatialization in other than general terms applicable to any novel. *A Brief Life* in fact makes a significant approximation to spatial *form*, in correlation to the victory over time that is the aim and the vaunted accomplishment of Brausen-Arce-Díaz Grey's fantasies. Existential time is contrasted with the timeless adumbrations of the artistic mind depicted; narrative time is spatialized in the ways already mentioned and in several other ways.

Defining spatial form in his well-known article, Joseph Frank described a poetics of fiction that unified "disparate ideas and emotions into a complex presented spatially in an instant of time."[3] The juxtaposition of disparate elements in the syntagmatic arrangement of the narrative yields the simultaneous perception of relationships between elements. The result, described by Frank (in Joyce, Proust and others), is the literary conversion of the time world of history into the timeless world of myth. Such a purpose is as visible in *A Brief Life* as it is in Proust's novel, and the effect of simultaneity is insinuated in a declaration of intent such as this: "Sometimes I wrote and at other times imagined the adventures of Díaz Grey, approximated Santa María through the foliage of the square and the roofs of the buildings near the river, wondered at the doctor's growing tendency to wallow over and over again in the same event, at the need—which was infecting me—to suppress words and situations, to attain a single moment that might express it all."

Frank's idea of simultaneity and mutually potentiating references within the work helps to reconstruct the spatial design of

A Brief Life, as does the notion of the "architectonic structure" of many modern works of fiction, catalogued in Sharon Spencer's extension of Frank's theory. One of the examples of a fully architectonic novel given by Spencer in *Space, Time and Structure in the Modern Novel* is Cortázar's *Hopscotch,* where she finds, among others, the following features: open structure (the intersection of art and life through self-reflexive apparatus and the deliberate rejection of the "frame" of the novel) and a montage consisting of the juxtaposition of units of varying lengths and perspectives that exhibit the novel's subject in non-narrative literary techniques (poetization, "essayism").[7] These features of *Hopscotch* are to some extent anticipated in *A Brief Life.*

The discourse of Onetti's novel moves from one zone to another of the schizoid self that grows out of Brausen's basic situation. This is accomplished by the juxtaposition of chapters with different settings or by fluid narrative alternation within a single chapter. Simultaneity develops the fundamental paradigm of Eros through the comparison and superimposition of the various love relationships. Derived from Brausen's wife and shown to be derived from her in the narration, Elena Sala retains the mysteriousness that has disappeared from "Gertrudis, known by heart." Part of Elena's mystery is her "whorehouse smile" but that connotation is more fully developed in the pairing of La Queca and Arce, (the prostitute and the kept man). This latter relationship, in turn, releases a repressed eroticism and violence which underlie Brausen's attitude toward Gertrudis. In one sense an atavistic replay of the first encounter between a younger Brausen and Gertrudis, the incident of Brausen's coupling with Gertrudis' younger sister Raquel is also a sordid and imperfect attempt at self-realization through the irresponsibility of exploitation, a game played by a cynical, experienced man with a naïve young woman. Adolescent woman and older man are more purely represented by the violinist and Díaz Grey in the final chapter. By comparing this couple with the other relationships, however, the reader may see through the purity and the sentimental aura of the final tableau and may suspect that its most decisive irony is that the Doctor and Annie Glaeson are merely beginning another fated cycle of love and disillusionment. (Other ironies undercut the couple's oblivion in the face of almost certain capture by the police for their part in shady drug deals, an oblivion paralleling Brausen's at the end of *his* plot, in the penultimate chapter, as he is about to be arrested.) This résumé of reflecting and refracting incidents, doubling effects among characters and other parallels need not be prolonged. Out of the process of simultaneous signification emerge mythic composites —archetypal Man, Woman, Love—within Onetti's circumscribed but subtly varied range.

The superimposition of variants within a limited range, the insistent wallowing "over and over again in the same event," amount to what Spencer calls closed structure. But *A Brief Life* also exhibits characteristics of the open structure. Its self-reflexivity reaches out of the novel's frame, even to the inclusion of a character named Onetti, reminding us that the brief life is the author's as well. The mutually reflecting final chapters—placing Brausen in his imagined Santa María purportedly with the irresponsibility and freedom of the fictional character and placing Díaz Grey in Buenos Aires—are ambiguous enough to be called open-ended.

A Brief Life does not approach the degree of textual miscellany to be found in *Hopscotch,* but Onetti's narrative is further varied by passages and chapters that blatantly estheticize the content by approxi-

mating other arts or, in one case, by entering into "essayism." Three examples are worth noting. In Chapter 8 of Part I, "Still Life," the narrative discourse is molded to the description of visual form. For the duration of two pages, the narration of what Brausen saw upon breaking into La Queca's apartment becomes a textual tour de force producing a short (still) life. Under the slow narrative glance, the random collection of objects takes on the effect of a painting minutely described. This feat of language creates a hiatus in the narrative sequence, just after the concept of the short life has been made explicit.

Blatant estheticization also detains, or diverts, the narrative in the first "Encounter with the Violinist." While Díaz Grey and Elena Sala are waiting for Annie's father, who may have news of the young man Elena is hunting for, the young girl practices a sonata. In one of the countless daydreams posited by the multiple consciousness of the novel, Díaz Grey mentally adds the missing piano accompaniment. The dialogue of instruments is translated into images and anthropomorphic emotions by the narration, again in a tour de force. Just as the music tries to speak ("She answered the piano's reticent discourse by saying, by trying to say, the inexpressible; . . ."), the passage stretches the function of the narrative and attempts to express music in words, and in those words the fusion of music and human sentiment. As in the still life, the manifest allusion to non-verbal art identifies the passage as a set piece and underscores the sublimating nature of daydreams.

After leaving Glaeson's, Elena and Díaz Grey pursue their manhunt at the provincial bishop's residence. The markedly symbolic chapter recounting their interview with the oracular churchman incurs something resembling Spencer's "essayism." In a sermonic, scholastic discourse, the bishop provides a taxonomy of desperate men: pure, impure, strong, weak, mixtures of these. The subject matter fits the border existential situations that predominate in the novel, but the sermon stands out as a spatially coordinated interpolation.

Onetti's self-reflexive probe of the power of fiction in A Brief Life suggests comparisons with such existentialist texts as Sartre's Nausea. Even more telling comparisons could be made with the work of Onetti's Argentine predecessors, Roberto Arlt and Borges. The title La vida breve is an homage not to DeFalla but to Arlt, the author of an El amor brujo (1932). In that novel and others, the erratic, innovative Arlt portrayed the powerless classes of River Plate urban society in their desperate recourse to illusion, doomed strategies of self-transcendense. While Onetti's novels prior to A Brief Life depicted fantasy-making within a rather Arltian "realist" perspective, A Brief Life takes an initially Arltian situation into a realm of Borgesian idealism, where fiction promises to prevail over experience, to refute time and historical circumstance. But as Borges' irony undermines the idealist claims of the texts of Ficciones (published before A Brief Life), Onetti's irony suggests limits to salvation through fiction. It is too simple to say, as Luis Harss has done, that A Brief Life is "a monument to evasion through literature."[4] The Santa María cycle of novels that have grown out of A Brief Life has retained the esthetic freedom established in the generative text, but a novel like The Shipyard (1961; English tr., N. Y.: Scribner's, 1968) can hardly be called "escapist." In it the Santa María setting becomes a space of grotesque caricature, a refraction of Argentine and Uruguayan social history, a realization of Arlt's partly unfulfilled project. ●

1. Sigmund Freud, Delusion and Dream and Other Essays (Boston: Beacon, 1956), p. 127.
2. Guido Castillo, "Muerte y salvación en Santa María," in En torno a Juan Carlos Onetti, ed. Lídice Gómez Mango (Montevideo: Fundación de Cultura Económica, 1970), pp. 66-67.
3. "Spatial Form in Modern Literature," in Joseph Frank, The Widening Gyre (Bloomington: Indiana Univ. Press, 1968), p. 9. First published in The Sewanee Review in 1945.
4. Luis Harss, Into the Mainstream (New York: Harper & Row, 1967), p. 186.

The Fragment as Disintegrated Unit

ZUNILDA GERTEL
Translated by Andrée Conrad

What's wrong with life isn't that it promises things it never gives,
but that it always gives them and then stops giving them.

A Brief Life

The most important novel of the 1950s from the Río de la Plata region, *A Brief Life* embodies that stage of technical and narrative evolution in the new novel of existential characters in which the text does not develop a psychological analysis but, rather, a way of being which in turn generates a disposition and an attitude toward life. Onetti's narrative does not postulate an ideology or an intellectual analysis of the ontological. Instead, the existential projection of the "I" is shown as a revelation within the literary experience as Onetti struggles with the signs imposed on him by literary tradition considered as ritual, not as reconciliation.

For its time, Onetti's writing signifies a radical change, a new narrative mode: the disintegration of language as the producer of text. In opposition to the Cartesian rational order of discourse, Onetti discovers the discontinuity of the fragment as a unit expressing the irrational. His *écriture* manifests this discontinuity in the linguistic structure of an "I" reincarnating and dispersing in its attempt to transcend the other. The alternation of fragment with narrative jump, of textual narrative with disjunctive shift, is imposed as a kind of montage, creating the space of this particular writing—a

ZUNILDA GERTEL is Professor of Spanish at the University of Wisconsin, Madison, and author of *Borges y su retorno a la poesía.*

space where imagination and fantasy must work to integrate the dissimilar elements. Onetti's writing tends toward that void of the "I" which is similar to the infinite space Maurice Blanchot speaks of in *L'espace littéraire.* As in Sartre's transcendence of the ego or as in Rimbaud's objectification in the famous phrase *Je est un autre,* so in Onetti's work the other, as object, is constituted by the dispersal and impersonality of the "I."

Starting from the rupture of rational order with a fissure that opens literary space, the first chapter of *A Brief Life* gives us the rhythm and the semantic of the complete story in a micro-narrative. In the solitude of his apartment, Brausen, the narrating character, recalls the routine of his unsuccessful life—his wife's illness, his boring work and his fear of losing it and of the consequent economic insecurity. In short, he experiences the onset of disintegration in the order of his day-to-day world. The motif of his wife's mutilated breast—she had recently undergone a mastecotomy—an image not yet presented but predicted in the passage, is obsessively repeated, prefiguring an end of love and the beginning of habit and boredom. The congruent motif of the probable loss of his job, accentuated by the impossibility of his completing the film script his advertising agency has commissioned alternates with the first motif. In turn, both are intercepted by a third: the voice of the unknown woman who has just moved into the apartment next door. " 'Crazy world,' the woman said once again. . . . When the woman's voice returned, I thought about the task of looking without disgust at the new scar Gertrudis would have on her breast, a round area, complicated, with a pattern of pink or red lines. . . ."

The interception of the fragmentary motifs is created by montage, and the consequent fragmentation of the text into a disintegrative whole is characteristic of both the minimal units and the total structure of the novel. The fragment imposes itself here as both *écriture* and as semantic. Specifically, Onetti's narrative operates through fragmented figures, especially the synecdoche—a part used to signify the whole—which implies a definite, elliptical fixation, but points to a broader meaning. The presence of the woman in the apartment next door to Brausen, for example, is fixed by synecdoches similar to narrative close-ups. Thus, it is not the *woman* herself who comes and goes, but rather her *voice* or her *laughter:* "three bursts of laughter; her laugh was the reverse of the anxious voice that stopped unexpectedly to mark the end of each phrase." Later Brausen will see how "her almost motionless shadow lengthened across the balcony tiles." Finally, when Brausen faces the woman for the first time, he discovers that "she is younger than her voice."

Synecdoche is a rhetorical figure expressing contiguity, but Onetti's abrupt combination of synecdoches serves both to fragment and integrate the text: thus, the inner space created between the part's synecdochial meaning and the whole's connotation brings to the surface of the text a semantic jump that in a single stroke disrupts the linear discourse. At the end of the first chapter, for example, the voice of the woman (La Queca) is joined by that of a man, also unknown (he will later turn out to be Ernesto), and these two people, both keys to the development of the novel, remain fixed in a fragmentary image, itself a synecdoche, when Brausen sees them in a kind of "medium shot" through the peephole in his front door: "As she continued to smile at the man, who was now showing me a gray shoulder and the dark brim of the hat on his head, her voice, hesitant, as if pressed into cotton to withstand the tenderness of pain, rose again and again to repeat that nothing could be changed."

Rejecting his daily routine governed by conventional order, Brausen invokes the freedom of his imagination as the only escape possible from his "I" in order to become the other. His imagination is projected towards dreams as a redemption from his inhibitions. His dreams, however, are created through a double perspective corresponding to a surrealist attitude in a double hierarchy of the irrational. According to the surrealists, man's dreams have two projections. On the one hand the will to dream transfers man's imagination into fantasy, the absurd dreaming which Baudelaire termed *hieroglyphique*. This dream represents the supernatural life and can be constantly changed and renewed. On the other hand, man's dreams appear within the realm of everyday life, but elements are combined in bizarre ways emphasizing the negative aspects of ordinary reality, conveying a degraded, chaotic, and even satanic sense of life—an infra-reality filled with cryptic meaning. That is what the surrealists called the "journey to hell." Inside his apartment, stretched out on his bed, in the physical inertia of long days occupied with dizzying mental activity, Brausen experiences both dream perspectives. His recalling the failures of his life—his separation from Gertrudis, the film script never completed, the loss of his job at Macleod Advertising, his estrangement from his friend Stein—all this sets off his total disavowal of the values established in his ordinary reality: "Slightly maddened, I played with the ampule, feeling my growing need to imagine and to draw close to me an indistinct doctor of forty years, the laconic and despairing inhabitant of a small city located between a river and a colony of Swiss farmers. Santa María because I had been happy there years ago, without reason and for twenty-four hours."

The story of Díaz Grey and Santa María, which Brausen had first thought of as a film script, emerges from the fiction and is transformed into Brausen's own fantastic, dreamed-story; that is, the supernatural side of his world: "Now the city is mine, together with the river and the ferry that moors at siesta time. Beyond is the doctor with his forehead leaning on the window; thin, sparse blond hair, the curves of his mouth worked by time and boredom; he looks out at a timeless noon. . . ." This surrealistic dreaming while awake is a free association of the mind invoking inner forces of the spirit which illuminate with intuitive purity an aspect of Brausen's everyday experience, transforming it into fantasy and the supernatural. Thus, the utopian doctor, Díaz Grey, is an idealization of Brausen, just as Elena Sala is of Gertrudis. Elena's husband—Horacio Lagos—and the gigolo, Andrés Owen, complete the creation of Brausen's double world, with his escape to the limitless and fantastic space of Santa María constituting a flight from his existential anguish: living the specific absurd in order to destroy the infinite absurd. This projection from Brausen's world onto the other, however, does not constitute a unification, but rather a fragmentation. The narrative disjunction implies Brausen's return to the closed reality of his apartment and to his transformation into Arce as he enters the degraded world of his neighbor, La Queca, the "undesirable woman" who is his mistress. Brausen convinces himself that he "had disappeared on the indeterminate day when my love for Gertrudis ended; I was subsisting on the double secret life of Arce and the country doctor."

Brausen's doubles, Díaz Grey and Arce, are respectively the protagonists of two opposite dreams which alternate in the fragmentary play within both spatial contexts: (1) the fantastic and absurd dream: the unreal and magic life that is latent in reality and (2) the dream that disintegrates Brausen's reality and becomes the infra-reality of his world. Both dreams—different planes of reality—represent the protagonist's obsessive conscience attempting to liberate his own self.

The meaning and boundaries of these opposite worlds—fantasy and freedom as well as degradation and imprisonment—are ex-

pressed in the double and opposed images of windows which stylistically function as synecdoche—as fragmentation of space. In the world of Santa María, there are two clear, wide windows in Díaz Grey's office: "I saw for certain, two large windows above the square: cars, church, club, market, drugstore, coffee shop, statue, trees. . . ." The view through the window is a panoramic image of escape to the dreamed world of Santa María and is expressed by fragmentation integrated with a paratactic syntax as an expansion of reflections within an endless space. In the opposite world of Brausen-Arce's reality, the small windows of the apartment always have the venetian blinds covering them, serving as separation and closure from the outside world: "the curtain of brown slats that hung rigidly between the afternoon sun and the bedroom." "I looked at the drawn blinds and quickly discovered that the disorder began there." Beyond the blinds, the night, the sky, and the rhythm of the seasons can be perceived as an attraction and a vertigo of the unattainable. Brausen knows they exist but is separated from them: "I convinced myself that I was simply planning to save myself in that night that was beginning beyond the balcony, exciting, with its intermittent gusts of warm wind."

While the windows of Santa María represent the wish for escape and freedom, the windows of the Brausen-Arce apartment function as a separated and closed space, like a dark wall which permits Brausen to know what occurs outside. Onetti presents the existential dilemma of the protagonist's being right next to the wall, perceiving the other side, but unable to jump over it. The absurdity of this paradox suggests that the dilemma will never be solved. ". . . And when we are determined and desperate, shut in by the height of the wall encircling us— so easy to leap over if it were possible to leap over it . . . when we perceive, however slightly, that only our own salvation can be a moral imperative, that only it is moral; when we succeed in breathing the natal air that vibrates and calls from the other side of the wall through an unforeseen chink. . . ."

In his radical anguish, Brausen realizes the frustration of existence and in his search for an escape, love and sex are his only hope for a short rebirth, for even a brief instant of life. Nevertheless, love is always an ephemeral encounter for Brausen. In vain he tries to recapture the image of a distant Gertrudis. As in other works by Onetti, in Brausen's world, women are specifically their bodies with the spontaneity of their adolescence deteriorated into the wasted and rigid form of maturity. Brausen likes to depict this physical deterioration in grotesque synecdoches: "Gertrudis mutilated . . . lay under the images of her failures." Mami, Stein's mistress, has "large blue eyes, myopic . . . dyed yellow hair . . . the fine veins below the layer of powder or rouge on the cheek that was beginning to sag." The body of Raquel, Brausen's distant, adolescent sister-in-law, is degraded by the shape of maternity: ". . . the stomach that came forward to a point over the thin parted thighs." On the other hand, Brausen perceives a transformed image of women in his dreamed worlds. In the utopian world of Santa María, women preserve their figures intact in the timelessness of empty space. If Elena is the recovered image of a distant Gertrudis, she is also the disintegrated reflection of many women: like a woman-rite, impenetrable in her mystery.

By opposition, La Queca is the degraded image of Gertrudis in Brausen's infra-world; hence, Brausen's vague idea of killing Gertrudis ultimately seeks to realize itself in La Queca, as if "in her he wanted to avenge all the insults he could possibly remember," in order to demonstrate in that way his "freedom as desperation" and achieve his salvation through the perfect crime. Paradoxically, it is within this degraded reality, on his first visit to La Queca's apartment, that the protagonist—totally alone—has a climactic experience. La Queca's apartment is the crazy, chaotic world which generates the other side of the surrealistic dream and the projection of Brausen's "I" into Arce: a sense of the existential abyss—a journey to hell—that is at the same time the entrance into a total experience with the certainty of achieving an authentic moment, of touching bottom, of nothing or everything: "I was calm and excited each time my foot touched the floor, believing that I was moving into the atmosphere of a brief life in which there was not enough time to become involved, to repent, or to age."

Onetti recreates this chaotic reality and its sense of abyss and void as well as that of the infinite instant by repeatedly using a fragmented enumeration and juxtaposed accumulation of elements: "To my right, at the foot of the empty silver frame with the splintered glass, I saw a one-peso bill and the shine of silver and gold coins. And in addition to all that I could see and forget, in addition to the worn-out tablecloth . . . there were, to the right near the edge of the table, packages of cigarettes either full and intact or open, empty, and crumpled; and also loose cigarettes, some stained with wine, bent, the paper torn by the swollen tobacco."

Brausen experiences the discovery of the hidden reality of things and feels his "I" pouring into them during an arrested moment, without beginning or end. In the hidden mystery of this crazy world of La Queca and her lovers, Brausen-Arce understands that he too is an initiate who is "inside the scandal," immersed in the fascination with the presence of "them," the invisible beings, small and impossible-to-find monsters who populate La Queca's reality, hallucinating and destroying her.

When Brausen-Arce is about to carry out his perfect crime and discovers that Ernesto has already done it, he feels that he is waking up, "not from this dream, but from another, incomparably longer, that included this one and in which I had dreamed I was dreaming this dream." Brausen-Arce, awakes from his dream, learns that Ernesto is the part of himself that has performed his, Brausen's, own action. If, according to Sartre's concept, the "I" is the object, and states of being and actions are also objects, Brausen-Arce and Ernesto are one and the same action, one and the same object. Namely, the death of La Queca. That is why Brausen identifies with Ernesto and why together they run from the police. This flight of the real characters will coincide with another,

La Vida Breve
Homenaje a Santa María

JOSE EMILIO PACHECO

Esta ciudad, de pronto, se inventa otro pasado.
El silencio está fuera de lugar.
Las casas son definitivamente de este mundo.
La noche se desploma sobre otra época.
El aire emponzoñado huele a campos antiguos.
Y todo se me vuelve aún más extraño
porque lo reconozco.
Porque ya de algún modo estuve aquí
(donde no he estado nunca).
Porque he perdido esta ciudad entrañable
que ahora recobro misteriosamente.
¿Y quién podrá decirme la verdad en este cauteloso fin del mundo?
¿Estoy vivo en mi vida pero me adentro en una fantasmagoria?
¿O todo, a fuerza de ser real,
me está volviendo un azorado fantasma?

similar flight: that of the fictitious beings of Santa María—Díaz Grey, Lagos and Owen, all involved in some dark drug trafficking. The fragmentary alternations of the opposite worlds intersect in a labyrinthine Santa María during carnival. This coincidence supports the fantasy within the fiction, creating a fantastic, dispersed space comprised of the make-believe of a twenty-four hour carnival where everything may occur and where the identity of characters changes repeatedly behind new and different masks.

Brausen disappears as narrator-character when both these dreamed worlds come together and he, as Brausen-Arce, enters the fictitious world of Santa María where the police come to arrest him. At this very moment Brausen confronts his existential attitude: "to be free, to be irresponsible toward others; . . . to achieve effortlessly a true solitude." That is, he confronts the freedom of his "I" as a void conscience, a depersonalization of the "I" into the object. In order to become the Other, Brausen is no longer Himself. At this point, Díaz Grey and the world of Santa María, which at the beginning of the novel sporadically rise up as Brausen's utopian dream, become the main motifs and textually take over the line of

development leading toward the final escape in the novel: the departure of Díaz Grey and the young female violinist in the dispersed space of a carnival dawn. Díaz Grey is now the first person of the story; he is the protagonist. At the same time, however, he is also a depersonalized, dispersed "I": Brausen projecting himself and suppressing himself in the other, feeling himself the sum of all the Brausens. The lady violinist is also Woman depersonalized—Gertrudis, Elena—the woman-rite. This explains why the narrator says at the beginning of the book when he creates Santa María: "because I was happy there years ago, without reason and for twenty-four hours."

The meaning of the "I" and its fragmentary projection in the other is supported by the narrative point of view. The first person permits an opening into the discourse through what Gerard Genette calls "planes of focalization." In *A Brief Life* the narrator is also the protagonist, but the two are not always on the same narrative plane. There is a double focalization of the first person. On the one hand, the external focalization of the narrator-witness who does not capture his own thoughts or internal monologues; on the other hand, the character

Translated by Alastair Reid

La Vida Breve
Homage to Santa María

Suddenly this city presents a different past.
Silence is out of place.
The houses are unquestionably of this world.
The night teeters over another age.
The festering air has the smell of ancient fields.
And everything becomes even stranger to me
because I recognise it.
For already in some sense I have been here
Because I have lost an intimacy with this city
which now mysteriously is returned to me.
And who could tell me the truth at this furtive end of the world?
Am I living in this world but entering an illusion?
Or is everything, because of being true,
becoming for me a disquieting ghost of itself?

who speaks for himself—no longer as narrator—in an internal focalization accentuated by the visual signs of writings, such as parentheses and quotation marks.

Onetti ably manipulates focalization of the first person—"I"-narrator, "I"-character—which is also a fragmentation of the "I" as well as a third person, "I"-he; that is, the projections of Brausen's doubles, in which the first and third persons intersect throught their impersonalness—what Benveniste would call the "non-person." Thus, the field of focalization is amplified in exploring the world of the other and a verbal game is created in opposition to the discourse of classical realism. This third plane of focalization ("I"-he) provides the greatest access to the narrative. For example, in one of the first fragmentary alternations in which Díaz Grey appears, the narrator says, "For some reason that I still ignored, the doctor wasn't wearing his white jacket at that moment; he [Díaz Grey] wore a gray suit, new, and was stretching black silk socks over his ankles. . . . I also had the woman [Elena], and I thought I had her forever. I saw her advance into the office, serious, and swaying slightly, in rhythm with her walk, a medallion with a photograph hung between her breasts. . . ." The first-person narrator refers to Díaz Grey in the third person; but, as the narrative advances, the narrator is ambiguously inserted as a participant, thus constituting the dual personality of Díaz Grey. The fragmentary oscillation of first and third person is a constant of the narrative game that embodies the transfer of the "I" to the object, and demonstrates it textually in both the *écriture* and in the discourse rather than in any intellectual logic.

This penetration of the "I" into the object achieves a singular meaning in Brausen's exploration of La Queca's apartment. Suddenly, in his discovery of their chaotic accumulation, objects which the narrator had only sensed take on magical, occult meaning. Brausen would say that "he was penetrating them without violence." Alone in the center of the silence, he experiences in one instant of brief life the vertigo of *being* those things. The projection of the "I" onto the other, or into the other, in turn signals the paradoxical fragmentation and dispersal of the "I," and the impossibility for Brausen of identifying it as a permanent unity. When Brausen returns, battered by Ernesto's attack, he says to himself: "I felt that I had preserved the essential so long as I continued calling myself Arce." Similarly when Brausen, the "man of only one woman," embraces La Queca, he reflects: "I squeezed her, sure that none of this was happening . . . sure that it was not I but Díaz Grey who was squeezing the body of a woman, the arms, the back and breasts of Elena Sala in the doctor's office at noon, finally."

If Brausen's attitude has its starting point in Sartre's sense of the existential condition —eradication and solitude; existence and not essence; liberty as desperation; an empty conception of the "I" and its projection onto the other—the gradation to the ultimate meaning of the novel conveys a transcendence of Sartre's conflict since Onetti's protagonist knows that there is something beyond his imprisonment. This search for hope is paradigmatic for the unique existential attitude in South American narrative, especially in the Río de la Plata region. In his existential conflict, the character perceives a hidden meaning of things as a capturing of the super-realistic. From the chaos of his frustration, beyond the walls of his enclosure, he detects a world that does not belong to him but that attracts him like a rite or a mystery, offering him the possibility of a brief, fragmentary opening.

The meaning of the novel is thus realized in the body of its *écriture*, in *the fragment*, a unit of disintegration implying the impossibility of permanent integration within the totality of the cosmos. The end of the novel is undetermined, but it is, undoubtedly, the affirmation of fantasy as reality in a limitless space of brief life: in the carnival dawn Díaz Grey and the woman violinist depart together in an instant of calm happiness. "I can go away in peace; I cross the small square and you walk at my side . . . without running from anyone, without wanting to meet anyone, dragging our feet a little, more from happiness than fatigue."

A Brief Life is the jump in hopscotch before *Hopscotch*—a fragment, a vertigo of what is attained and lost in the moment of attainment, an instant that disintegrates but whose particles remain vibrating in the air, repeated in the rite of the seasons, in the imperturable rhythm of time.

Anguish of the Ordinary

GEORGE LEVINE

By coincidence, I was in the midst of re-reading *Madame Bovary* when I was given Juan Carlos Onetti's *A Brief Life*. Strikingly, the two novels began blurring into each other as I alternated between them: the century and the continent that separate them do not disguise their cousinship. Not that there is—or that it is necessary to imply— direct literary influence, but both novels occupy space in the Western tradition of literary realism that thickens with the paradoxes inevitably created by the attempt to speak truth about reality.

The discipline to which Flaubert subjected himself is closely analogous to the disciplines of Onetti's narrator. Flaubert's personal salvation seemed to depend on the most precise and particular notation of objects. Such notation was meant to purge both the hateful bourgeois reality it described and the catastrophic, romantic dreams of Emma Bovary. Ironically, however, the very intensity of Flaubert's notation begins to invest objects with significances that remove them from the ordinary world in which he desperately labors to place them. Object becomes symbol and resonates with new possibilities of feeling. The hiss of Emma's corset string or the

GEORGE LEVINE teaches English at Livingston College, Rutgers University. Author of *The Boundaries of Fiction*, he is currently at work on a book about realism in the nineteenth-century English novel.

beaded sweat on her bare shoulders is more passionately evocative than any of Emma's fantasies; we are in danger of substituting one dream for another. Flaubert imagined that his dream was better than Emma's, since it confronted what he imagined to be the worst and took shape in words so precise that they seemed to master the hideousness that always threatened to destroy him.

Juan María Brausen, Onetti's narrator, lives in a world of objects so intensely and profusely perceived that there is barely space for him. Unlike Emma Bovary, but like Flaubert, he begins disenchanted. The romantic dream is reduced in him to the merest possibility that through the objects themselves it might be possible to enter a world and a self alternative to the hideous and repetitive bourgeois reality. But since the rules of Onetti's novel turn out to be pretty much the same as the rules within which Brausen's imagination must work (to reject the rules is to reject what Flaubert knew a century before), the alternative threatens to be pretty much the same as the original.

Onetti, that is, includes both Flaubert's subject *and* his attempted solution within his novel. If there be any solution to the ordinariness, the inevitable decay, the hard trivia and terrible sense of loss that make up the realist's "ordinary life," it seems to lie not in Flaubert's kind of imagination of objects, but in the imagination of that kind of imagination. We are threatened with a kind of infinite regress into an unattainable clarity of reality, as fiction becomes more and more self-conscious about its fictionality. Like Flaubert, we must see that the romantic and religious literature shaping Emma's consciousness is inadequate. Like Brausen, we must see that the kind of assertion of the ordinary towards which Flaubert moved is inadequate since it contains within itself a dream of control that contradicts its own impulses. Like Onetti, we must come to terms with the double inadequacy and perhaps return the hard way to a dream of freedom earned through that double recognition.

All of this is exquisitely tortured. So, too, *A Brief Life* is a book astonishingly rich in the anguish of the ordinary and in Chinese boxes of illusion. It contains almost three novels-worth of elaborations of these paradoxes—narratives that move in and out of each other, every one thick with particularities of life and decay. It is at once an exhaustingly intellectual novel, full of speculations about language and illusion and dreams of freedom, and an old-fashioned, heartbreakingly realistic rendering of loss and pain and isolation. It is both a naturalistic novel dwelling remorselessly on a slow descent into total loss and failure—like Emma's story, or Nana's—and a Beckett-like record of nothing happening. Part of the illusion is that we are made to feel that something is happening, but it is always and only Brausen's mind struggling to enact itself in action or in words.

Brausen is a neuraesthenic ventriloquist. We meet him first as he counterpoints two not-quite present realities as though they were present. Through the wall of his apartment he hears sounds from next door, where a woman has just moved in. But they become more than sounds: "I imagined her mouth moving in front of the refrigerator's cold vapor and vegetable odors as she faced the curtain of brown slats that hung rigidly between the afternoon sun and the bedroom, obscuring the disorder of recently arrived furniture." That imagined reality somehow participates in Brausen's hope "for a vague miracle that would bring springtime to me." But the girl next door is a "chippy," and the "vegetable odors"—the imagined decay—are juxtaposed against Brausen's imagination of his wife, who will soon be coming back from breast surgery: "A scar can be imagined as an irregular cut made on a rubber cup with thick walls, containing a motionless substance, pinkish, with bubbles on the surface, and that may give the impression of being liquid if we make the lamp that illuminates it sway back and forth."

The Brausen situated between these two women—Gertrudis, the wife whose breast amputation is a physical analogue to the death of their relationship that had preceded it, and La Queca, the chippy, whose chubby sexuality is a pathetic business substitute for the loves she will never have—

begins inventing other worlds where "spring" may be possible. Indeed, the novel will end twice—just as Carnival ends—for at least two of Brausen's later incarnations, in an incipient spring with the masquerades over and the Brausen surrogates freed into the inevitable temporal failures, into "a final disenchantment without complexity."

But that disenchantment is only possible through the complexities of invented alternatives. To avoid the implications of the loss of his wife and of his job, he tries to write a screenplay that will bring him the success he has always missed. And he invents Díaz Grey of Santa María, who quickly becomes one of the novel's narrators; shortly after, as the two narratives proceed, Brausen turns himself into La Queca's "man," Arce, separates from his wife, and pretends to open his own office, rented to him by a man named Onetti, amiable and indifferent, at whose back he stares while he imagines Díaz's story.

Thus, in the life of the novel, and in the life of his mind, Brausen, a displacement of Onetti, is displaced continuously, though erratically. Díaz Grey's story begins clearly enough as Brausen's strenuous and conscious effort to invent it. He longs to achieve "the long initial sentence that would return me to life again." But Díaz Grey takes on his own life and possesses much of the narrative, except that his narrative falls into traps such that it must frequently be cancelled or altered. Brausen *can* alter the narrative, which comes to us with a kind of naturalistic fidelity that makes the manipulations shocking; Onetti cannot quite alter Brausen's narrative.

But the novel as a whole becomes a quest for a fiction that will, eventually, cancel itself out, will move outside the whoredom, the vegetable decay, the cancerous corruption, the personality defined by inadequate memories and impossible hopes. To be sure, the quest is doomed, and all the desperate turnings of the novel reflect something like Flaubert's romantic despair at the limitations of the quotidian. At one point, Brausen tells his wife that the problem is people's belief that "they're condemned to a single life until death. And they are only con-

demned to a soul, a manner of being."

Indeed, the ultimate coherence of the book depends upon this final limitation, Brausen's condemnation to a soul. (He, surely, is not condemned to a single life.) Although they are invented to overcome the deadly repetitiveness of domesticity, the narratives echo each other in ways that imply inescapable, psychological repetition. Like Díaz Grey, Brausen is attracted to a woman, Elena Sala, who is addicted to morphine and to a handsome young Englishman—in both of which addictions she is supported by her husband Lagos. Elena seems an alternative to Brausen's Gertrudis. Lagos seems another, more heroic version of Brausen's friend Stein—himself married to an ex-whore—who manages to be sentimental, successful, duplicitous and endearing. Arce, Brausen's surrogate with La Queca, moves into an alien world totally opposed to the middle-class world of Brausen next door. He treats La Queca as a pimp would, and settles easily into a brutal control, apparently waiting for the opportunity to kill a violent young friend, Ernesto, who had once beaten him. As Brausen himself, Brausen fails in his relationship with Gertrudis' sister, as he had failed with Gertrudis.

All the stories are of relationships thwarted, achievements forestalled, moments repeated. At one point, Brausen wonders at Díaz Grey's "growing tendency to wallow over and over again in the same event, at the need—which was affecting me —to suppress words and situations, to attain a single moment to express it all." Elena Sala is cast out of the story, returns, is killed, returns again. Neither Díaz Grey nor Brausen can control her. Arce plans to shoot La Queca. Ernesto does it. Brausen is resolved to suppress Díaz Grey, but he leads Ernesto to the real city he had imagined as Díaz Grey's home, and Díaz Grey returns. As Brausen attempts to protect Ernesto (hence to become master of the alien), so Lagos and Díaz Grey attempt to protect the Englishman who (not Díaz Grey) kills Elena. Both attempts fail.

Nothing can succeed, nothing but the extraordinarily imagined moments on the way to failure. In all of his incarnations,

Brausen's "manner of being" persists. Nothing happens but what must. Brausen, Díaz Grey, Arce are all Flaubertian realists who somehow know that the objects participating in delay and occasioning failures are the only way out. The intractable reality that Flaubert imposed on his Emma is not merely, as Brausen knows, intractably out there.

The realist's "object," the artist's "word," the real world's "self" are all closely related. Lagos, like Brausen, looks for the saving sentence: "the spontaneous surrender to a moment we have always longed for. When we repeat the same sentence, and this sentence doesn't lose its novelty and serves to explain everything." The novel seeks the sentence, the word, that will pare away all conventions buffering us from the "object," from the experience, that protect us by ideas about past and future from ourselves. To transform himself into Arce, Brausen works through objects. "And I'm going to fondle them with such an intensity of love that one by one they won't be able to resist me." And we realize that from the first page, this is what Brausen and Onetti have been doing. The alien objects—dead leaves, hexagonal machine nuts—have been fondled, loved, penetrated, and through them the self is born. The realist ideal of recording commonly available reality becomes the means of transcendence into a new self.

In one of the most remarkable and beautiful passages in the novel, we are given a "part of the history of Díaz Grey [that] was never written." At a crucial point in an interview with a bishop, Brausen gives himself the option of imagining the bishop's talk as "amiable buffoonery" or, for Elena and Díaz Grey, "truth and revelation." The story branches off, depending for its movement on how a carving of a pensive angel behind the bishop is perceived. The angel seems to smile as the bishop forces Díaz Grey (and Brausen? and Onetti?) to see that "only God is eternal." A commonplace, to be sure, but crucial in the light of the book's effort to forestall time. "And," says the bishop, "the debased conscience that permits [us] to accept the capricious, dismembered, and complacent sensation that [we] call the past, that permits [us] to cast off lines of hope,

and to correct mistakes that [we] call time and the future, is only, even admitting it, a personal consciousness." To this consciousness, eternity is not available. But, says our curiously existential and not altogether trustworthy bishop (the angel has winked), "I will kiss the feet of him who may comprehend that eternity is now, that he himself is the only end, that he must accept and strive to be himself, simply that, without need of reasons, at all times and against all opposition, living in abject poverty through passion, forsaking memory and imagination." The chapter ends with the only moment in which Díaz Grey and Elena are allowed compassion for each other. She "lay softly on the bed: nothing more than a precarious symbol of the world, of her relation with the world, unimprovable because of the circumstances, indispensable for the charitable act." But none of this was "written."

The terrible contradictions are all in this scene. Onetti had to write it and have Brausen tell us that it was not written. Elena, the imagined woman, is in her reality an alien object whose separation is a condition of the rare charity. Forsaking memory and imagination, the object is time-bound, alien, a condition of selfhood and eternity.

A Brief Life is, at last, an overwhelming and very beautiful book. It is not easy about that "eternity" of the bishop, but it knows how to love objects, how to feel loss and pain, how to confront the damaging limitations of mere personality. It is a drama of the creation of the unattainable sentence that Flaubert began writing a century before, that Faulkner (one of Onetti's favorites) could never quite finish. The disgust with the real which Flaubert had to overcome in order to exorcise his romantic self is transformed into a passionate acceptance of the ordinary and of the impossibility of writing it. The real, more intensely present, is perhaps less real than Flaubert dreamed he knew. The book's epigraph is from Walt Whitman, the American visionary realist, and it invokes "something escaped from the anchorage and driving free."

 FOCUS

Machado de Assis

A serious Sterne?
A comic Flaubert?
A Borges born in 1839?
No. A Brazilian dead in 1908,
but disturbingly alive in 1976,
delightfully ahead of his time.
With works in thirteen languages,
from his own Portuguese
to everyone else's Esperanto,
including six novels and
a collection of short stories
in English translation,
Machado de Assis was aware
of the precise anomaly
of his future position as
one of the greatest writers
in Latin American letters:
"Properly speaking, I am a deceased
writer, not in the sense
of one who has written and
is now deceased, but in the sense
of one who has died
and is now writing."
A very contemporary view
of the writer, espoused
by one of his first alter egos,
Braz Cubas, it celebrates life
as a form of elaboration:
a text in continual motion:
Machado de Assis.

Thomas Colchie
Guest Editor

Chronology

Compiled by
RUSSELL G. HAMILTON

═══════════════════════

1839. Joaquim Maria Machado de Assis is born June 21 on a country estate in the village of Livramento, Rio de Janeiro; he is the first child and only son of tenant-worker parents Francisco José de Assis, mulatto, freedman, housepainter, and Maria Leopoldina Machado da Câmara, a Portuguese washerwoman from the Azores.

1845. Joaquim Maria's only sister, Maria, dies just short of her fourth birthday.

1849. His mother dies of tuberculosis leaving behind a thin, sickly child given to occasional, unexplained seizures, later diagnosed as epilepsy. Years later, Machado would confide to a friend that he did more justice to Nature than She did to mankind.

1854. Maria Inês da Silva, about whom little is known, becomes Joaquim Maria's stepmother. His father's second marriage coincides with Machado's leaving home for the court city of Rio. Contrary to popular belief, the young boy does not receive his early schooling at his stepmother's knee; he is a virtual autodidact who teaches himself French and devours the works of European masters as well as those of Brazilian authors. As if in defiance of his puniness, he gives himself over to arduous labor, both

RUSSELL G. HAMILTON, Professor of Portuguese, Brazilian and Afro-Portuguese literature at the University of Minnesota, is the author of *Voices from an Empire: A History of Afro-Portuguese Literature.*

physical and intellectual. During this period he holds a variety of jobs, including that of clerk in a stationery store. Then he meets Francisco de Paula Britto, a typographer and the owner of a bookstore. By befriending the young Joaquim Maria and employing him as a proofreader Paula Britto assures his own measure of immortality.

1855. At the age of sixteen, Joaquim Maria inaugurates his literary career inauspiciously with the poem *"A palmeira"* (The Palm Tree), published in the magazine *Marmota fluminense.*

1859. Machado's special wit begins to emerge. In a theatre review published in *O espelho* he writes: "On Monday the National Opera opens with *Pipelot,* an opera in three acts with music by Ferrari and poetry by Mr. Machado de Assis, a close friend of mine, my alter ego, for whom I have deep affection but about whom I am unable to offer any opinion."

1864. At the age of twenty-five, Machado de Assis, in his own words, "leans on life's windowsill, eyes on the river that flows by, the river of time, not only in contemplation of the waters' perennial course but also in hopes of sighting, either up or downstream, the gold and sandalwood galleon with silk sails that will carry me to a certain enchanted island."

On April 22 Machado's father dies and receives a pauper's burial. By this time Machado has lost touch with his family; but in dry, precise language he dedicates his first volume of poetry, *Crisálidas* (Chrysalides), "to the memory of Francisco José de Assis and Maria Leopoldina Machado de Assis, my parents."

1867. Having left the *Diário do Rio* to become the Director of Government publications, on March 16, by order of the Emperor Dom Pedro II, Machado is a made a Knight of the Order of the Rose as a result of his reputation as theater critic, poet and dramatist. He thus ironically assumes a position among the bourgeoisie of the Second Empire, or as one writer has put it, "Machado, the public official, enters silently into the aristocracy."

Ensconced in secure respectability Machado readies himself to satirically depict the bourgeoisie of Rio de Janeiro; and the fact that this is his adopted social class—or better, the class that adopts him—makes his observations only sharper. Even as aristocrat, Machado is ever the interloper.

1869. On November 12 Machado marries Carolina Augusta Xavier de Novais, a Portuguese woman who would share his successes and his melancholy.

1872. He publishes *Ressurreição* (Resurrection), an anti-romantic novel written in the romantic manner. One of Machado's biographers, Barreto Filho, wrote of this first novel that "for the time being Machado desires to travel the beaten path and he refuses to heed his interior demon's invitation to another adventure."

1874. With the publication of his second novel, *The Hand and the Glove* (The University Press of Kentucky), the tension between romanticism and realism increases.

1876. *Helena*, his third novel, is published.

1878. *Iaiá Garcia*, the fourth and last novel of his initial phase, moves Machado closer to Flaubertian realism and toward that unique, if slightly disjointed, position he was to assume in Brazilian literature. Still, as the Brazilian poet Manuel Bandeira so aptly stated, "If Machado had disappeared at that time he would have left works in which poetry and prose were balanced on the same level of mediocrity." In April, Machado criticizes the Portuguese master of realism, Eça de Queirós. He attacks Eça's acclaimed novel *Cousin Basilio* on the grounds that it is pornographic in its sexual explicitness and artificial in its conclusion. What seems to be prudish indignation is really Machado's interior demon struggling to surface. As he prepares for the novels of his second phase, Machado finds himself "dueling against the mighty swords of naturalism and positivism." At this point, he is beset by a mysterious illness.

1879-1880. Some influential critics seem not to understand his fifth novel *Epitaph of a Small Winner* (Noonday Press), published first in installments in the magazine *Revista brasileira* and then in book form. Machado's demon arrives. Oddly enough, by going back to the 18th-century wit of Sterne and Swift, in defiance of contemporary trends, Machado manages to be disturbingly ahead of his time. Notwithstanding the shock displayed by a number of conservative literati, Machado's audacious novel is destined to become the cornerstone of Brazilian realism.

1801-1882. If 1881 is an important year for Machado the novelist, it is likewise a landmark date for Machado the short-story writer. The long short story or novella, *The Psychiatrist* (University of California Press), while not generally considered one of Machado's demon arrives. Oddly enough, an astonishing satire of positivist scientism; and the story serves in this chronology as a rallying point for the Pascalian aphorism that "men are so necessarily mad that not to be mad would amount to another form of madness." Rather than progressively ascending toward perfectability, people are seen by Machado as being caught up in a circular repetition of ignorance and stupidity unworthy of humankind's highest aspirations. Machado seems to align himself with all the imperfect madmen in the outside world and thus he accepts humankind in all its non-mad madness.

1891. "To the victor go the potatoes," Machado's parody of the Darwinian dictum "survival of the fittest," sums up, in comic fashion, his sixth novel *Quincas Borba: Philosopher or Dog?* (Noonday Press). This sequel to *Epitaph of a Small Winner* revolves around the provincial schoolteacher Rubião who is the sole heir of Quincas Borba, the fictitious author of *The Philosophy of Humanitism*. Borba's book is an outrageous parody of Auguste Comte's Positive philosophy and its application to Brazilian reality. Along with Quincas Borba's money, Rubião inherits his benefactor's dog who bears his master's name. (Comte prized the dog as man's greatest accomplishment in the domestication of animals.)

In July, Machado's godmother dies and thus the last human link with his childhood disappears. Machado returns to Livramento to salvage a brick from his demolished boyhood home. About this sentimental act Luis Viana Filho, writes "to hide it [his past] is easy; to forget it, however, is impossible."

1894. Deocleciano Mártir, a staunch supporter of the young Republic (declared in 1889), accuses Machado of being an enemy of the regime and a monarchist conspirator. According to rumor, Machado refused to remove a portrait of the old Emperor from his office wall. This is one of several incongruities that surround Machado's public life; he is also accused of being an anti-abolitionist who refuses to defend the downtrodden group from which he himself is only two generations removed. Lúcio de Mendonça, a stalwart of the republican press, rebukes Mártir in the inflated journalistic style of the day:

Who is this man (Machado)? Everybody knows, except perhaps Mr. Deocleciano Mártir. He is a product of himself, *ex se natus*, to use Tacitus' expression; an obscure, anonymous artist, a typographer, then a proofreader, after that a reporter, next a chronicler, a feuilletonist, a poet, and then the undisputed leader of Brazilian literature. Just this: a national reputation gained little by little, step by step, day by day, in modesty, in perseverance, and in labor, in honorable labor for his daily bread, and in study and the noble effort to gain wisdom and glory.

As for Machado's supposed denial of his African ancestry, it is true he does not contribute to a body of pamphletary, *Uncle Tom's Cabin*-like literature produced in Brazil at the time. But in at least four of his novels and in several short stories he makes caustic, though subtle allusions to slavery.

1896. December 15 marks the founding of the Brazilian Academy of Letters to which Machado de Assis is elected the first president.

1899-1900. *Dom Casmurro* (University of California Press), Machado's seventh and, for many, his best novel is printed in Paris in 1899 and distributed in Brazil the following year. As does Braz Cubas in *Epitaph*, Bento Santiago, the protagonist of *Dom Casmurro*, sets out to write his autobiography and, in telling his story, relates how he grew into that cynical middle-aged man nicknamed Sir Morose, or Mr. Grumpy, as some prefer to translate Dom Casmurro. With irony and an often humorous skepticism that pass for philosophical musings on life's vicissitudes, Casmurro subtly defends his arid soul. What is experimental in *Epitaph* becomes innovative in *Dom Casmurro*.

1902. With his great *trilogy* of novels behind him, Machado de Assis, the public servant, mingles in the world of bureaucracy as Director of the Secretariat of Industry.

1904. In *Esau and Jacob* (University of California Press), his next-to-last novel, Machado returns to the third-person, omniscient narrative used in *Philosopher or Dog?*, except that in the former, the narrator Ayres also figures in the story. Here, wit gives way to more reflective modes.

On October 20, Carolina dies, leaving her husband to the meditative quietude of his alter ego, Ayres.

1908. His own death near, Machado awaits the proofs of his final novel, *Counselor Ayres' Memorial* (University of California Press). A sequel to *Esau and Jacob*, the story is a memoir in which *saudade* (that intranslatable Luso-Brazilian "nostalgia") predominates. For many, the venerable, benevolent Ayres is an autobiographical character who indulges in Proustian reminiscences that convey the stoicism of a man resigned to human destiny. *The Psychiatrist's* Dr. Bacamarte had vainly sought the unity of the soul; Ayres finally illustrates the equilibrium of the soul. On September 29, 1908, Joaquim Maria Machado de Assis dies, leaving behind a vastly illusive progeny: his own fiction. ◐

The Essential Machado de Assis

ALEXANDER COLEMAN interviews WILLIAM L. GROSSMAN,
translator of *Epitaph of a Small Winner,* on New York University's
Sunrise Semester television series (1972).

*I want to ask your feelings regarding the
central concern in Machado's Epitaph of a
Small Winner. I wonder if there's some con-
necting link which brings together all the
disparate chapters in the work and which
gives it a single vision.*

It seems to me that the central feature of
this book and indeed of most of Machado's
works, at least those written in his maturity,
is his ridicule of the superficial in human
life, in human conduct, in human thought—
the inauthentic, the trivial. This comes out
again and again in many chapters, for example in "The Muleteer," which is prac-
tically a short story in itself. When Braz is
coming back from Coimbra, he is almost
killed, or so it seems to him, and he's rescued by a muleteer. Now for a moment Braz
has deep feeling. He understands that this
man, at some peril to himself, has rescued
him. Braz is filled with generosity and wants
to give him a gold piece. But how long does
it last? About two seconds—then Braz falls
to his customary level of superficiality and
ends up giving him a few pennies. And this
sort of thing is not confined to Braz's experience. Take that old businessman, Viegas,
who is dying. He obviously has only a few
minutes to live—and what does he do? Does
he pray? Is he filled with awe at the mystery
he is about to face? Nothing so profound
as that. He bargains on the price of some
real estate, right up to the last moment.

*I think the chapter ends with the death rat-
tle, doesn't it?*

He's saying "f . . . f . . . for . . ."—trying to
say "forty."

*Is this related to the whole problem of ego-
ism in Machado?*

Yes. I think that egoism is identified with
superficiality. So the egocentric approach,
ridiculed a great deal by Machado, really
doesn't represent a greatly different field.
It's an aspect, I think, of the inauthentic.

*I agree. I'm using the edition first published
in 1956, the paperback, now in the eighth
printing. How do you explain that this book
not only has been kept in print but also
still has a magnetic effect for the younger
generation?*

That's the fascinating thing. I think that
Machado appeals a great deal to young people because of his hatred of hypocrisy. The
hypocrisy that one finds in his characters
is so pervasive that it's hard to point out
one example rather than another. But I think
the episode of Braz and the money is a
good one. You remember, Braz finds some
money and, being in his own opinion an
honest man, he returns it. His image of himself is that of an honorable man. Then he
finds a larger sum of money and doesn't

return it. Pure hypocrisy. And if you don't mind my giving another example, take Dr. Villaça. He's not a major character; he's the extemporizer at that party given by Braz's father when Napoleon is defeated. Someone praises him for his wonderful style. He replies with ostensible modesty, "Ah, you say that only because you never heard Bocage." Well, Bocage was a very famous Portuguese poet, perhaps the greatest extemporizer of his day. Then what does Villaça go on to say? "I competed with Bocage once and the applause was tremendous." You see, he is really lifting himself, not expressing modesty, by comparing himself to Bocage.

But the savage attack against hypocrisy is always done with a considerable amount of urbanity.

Yes, yes. That's right. And there, I think, the counter-culture of the sixties, which persists to some extent into the seventies, has a lot to learn from Machado. Machado's attack on hypocrisy was the attack of a civilized man. He was, as you say, urbane, whereas the younger people so often are atavistic in their approach. The notion of violence would horrify Machado, you see. He was a profoundly civilized man.

And yet no one questioned the foundations of society more than he.

That's right. Like the counter-culture of today, he hated the dishonesty in the Establisment and the inferior values. But the way he got at them was to kid the pants off them. And, at least in many circles and for many purposes, that can be more incisive, more effective, more long-lasting. than breaking windows or setting off bombs.

You know, there's a book called Madness and Civilization *by Michel Foucault, a French sociologist, and he comes to the conclusion that really, the insanity is not within the asylum but outside the asylum. Now, you've translated this marvelous novella (I think we'd call it),* The Psychiatrist. . . .

Yes, Machado has a pre-Freudian psychiatrist—the first in Brazil—given authority by a municipality to place the abnormal in an institution, an asylum. Well, his standards are rather naïve. He goes looking for a man whose behavior indicates a lack of balance. He finds a man who is terribly obsequious and he says, "Well, this is certainly abnormal behavior," and he puts him in the asylum. And he does the same to a man who is overly proud of his house. And so on.

Mild eccentricities.

Yes. Well, mild from the point of view of psychopathology, perhaps. But this is a social psychiatrist; and if a person departs strikingly from the accepted norm he considers this to be unbalanced, abnormal behavior and puts him in the asylum. The trouble is that before long almost all the population of the community finds itself locked up in the asylum. And then the psychiatrist, being a man of science, says, "Well, they must be the norm because they represent the bulk of the population, and the well-balanced people must be the abnormal ones." So he lets all those people out and he looks around for some well-balanced people to put in. There are very few of these. He finds a few and he puts them in the asylum. But he can't cure them. He plays on their little defects, magnifies them, and gets these people to be ill-balanced until they are . . .

Sufficiently abnormal.

So that they meet the norm. And then he lets them out. But then there's nobody in the institution. So, the poor fellow, he has to look around for a man who is incurably normal, incurably well-balanced. He finds only one. And so, as an honest scientist, he locks *himself* up in the asylum. I think the moral is fairly clear.

What was Machado's general attitude toward organized religion—or to unorganized religion, for that matter?

Well, he was critical of organized religion.

He has clergymen among his characters and often depicts them in a light that shows their lack of spirituality. So far as theology is concerned, Machado seems to have been agnostic. I think he never could accept the idea of a Christian or Judeo-Christian God. On the other hand, he was a deeply spiritual man and that's why he rejected the superficial in life, the inauthentic, the egocentric.

So he is very much a pessimist, a very melancholy temperament—certainly in this book and in some of the short stories and in The Psychiatrist. *But do you think it's the kind of melancholy which is self defeating?*

No, I don't think so. Machado was not a suicidal type. First of all, although he rejected everything mundane, he always, I think, had his eye on the profound as something worth reaching for. And sometimes he found it. In this last novel (*Counselor Ayres's Memorial*), for example, one thing that readers almost always remember is the relationship between the middle-aged or tending-to-be-elderly couple. Here are people who have gone beyond sexual passion, at least in any blatant and conspicuous aspect, on to a kind of profound respect and relationship of kindness toward each other. And Machado does not ridicule them. He *does* ridicule sexual passion, as between Virgilia and Braz. What does it lead to? Nothing. It's always superficial. But genuine affection, I think, represented for Machado a clue to profundity.

So in that sense passionate love, romantic love, is almost a key to personal disaster. But what about the possible sources of this book? I mentioned Tristram Shandy *in a previous lecture. What about Shakespeare? Machado's affection for* Hamlet?

You spoke of the pessimism that might lead to suicide. Machado's pessimism was a rich pessimism because it had a spiritual base. not unlike, in some respects, Hamlet's; because when Hamlet expresses his pessimism —"How weary, stale, flat and unprofitable seem to me all the uses of this world!"—it's a rich expression of a rich pessimism. I don't know if that's a very meaningful phrase, but perhaps you see what I mean.

I certainly do. But it is curious, you know, the vision of love and womanhood in someone like Marcella and someone like Virgilia. Eugenia is the unique case of a remarkable human being within the novel. After all, Braz is not especially remarkable; Eugenia is.

Eugenia is candid; she's an honest woman. She's a quiet woman, quiet not only in that she doesn't speak much but one thinks that she's quiet in her inner being too. Braz is volatile. He's egocentric—not by doctrine— he's casually egocentric; Braz has no doctrine. He's flotsam and jetsam. He's Everyman. But Eugenia is not. Eugenia is quiet. She's the still water that runs deep. And therefore she has to be pushed aside; she cannot play any part in Everyman's life.

Do you think Braz Cubas is Machado de Assis?

In personality he's remote from Machado. But the philosophy and lack of philosophy that he expresses both have their roots in Machado's point of view. Machado's pessimism is brought out clearly through Braz in both word and action, but I think Machado's profundity comes through mostly by implication.

How would you interpret the philosophy of Quincas Borba and his final demise, which of course is a complete collapse into insanity?

Well, I think that through Quincas Borba, the "philosopher," Machado was attacking two trends in philosophy in his day. One was the reflection of Darwinianism in the idea of the superman, which must have seemed like so much piffle to Machado. This was just egocentricity carried to the nth degree. And even though Machado wrote this book, I think, a little before Nietzsche's major works, still it was in the air. More specifically and importantly, I think he was attacking the philosophy of a Frenchman named Comte, who made humanity the thing to be worshiped. To worship humanity, to deify humanity, must have seemed to Machado the absolute height of absurdity—humanity with its terrific inadequacy, its inability to have profound experience for more than a fleeting second.

Now, how did you find out about Machado? I mean, after all, you are the man who first translated a novel by Machado de Assis into English.

I'm glad you asked me that question, as the professors say. Well, I went down to Brazil in 1948 at the invitation of the Brazilian Government to help found a university there. I was to organize and teach in one of the departments. I lectured in Portuguese, but my Portuguese at the start was pretty poor. So I asked my friends, "Where can I get a really good Portuguese style? Who is your best writer?" And they said, "Machado de Assis." So I read Machado and it was a revelation to me. To stumble on a master is a great experience.

And then you set to work translating the book.

That's right. It took me longer to translate it than it took Machado to write it. I took the responsibility very seriously. I went through the whole book with a Brazilian friend, and when I didn't trust him I consulted another Brazilian friend. And then I published an edition of the translation at my own expense in Brazil to circulate to Brazilian scholars and get their comments. Then I came with the final manuscript to the United States and—incredible!—two big publishers turned it down.

It is astonishing because, after all, this is a work that, as I say, is now in its eighth printing. It is a work that I have taught at New York University, and the students have been utterly overwhelmed by the contemporaneity of Machado de Assis. The savagery, of course—the savagery of the attack and the social criticism—is very much a

part of the ethic that is motivating many students today.

Yes, very true. The fact is that, in a sense, those publishers were not altogether mad, because Machado de Assis infuriates some readers. As a matter of fact, Machado de Assis, if you read him as he apparently wanted to be read, is pointing the finger at the reader all the time. And some readers don't like that.

Agreed: The reader wants to deflect the view. I mean, the reader is delighted to see the character satirized. But I don't think that the reader is constantly willing to have the author point his finger at him. The reader doesn't find himself included in the game, so to speak.

That's if he's superficial; that's right. But then if the reader really gets the point, he begins to squirm, unless he's man enough to take it, of course, and then it's a joy to him. He begins to squirm and he may put Machado aside when he begins to suspect what Machado is after. And Machado is blunt about it sometimes. The only thing is, he's so good-natured about it that maybe he'll get away with it. For example, he says at one point, "You know what's wrong with this book, reader? You are." And I was very much surprised once, watching a television program with Henry Morgan, the humorist, who has a kind of sarcasm not far from Machado de Assis'.

What did he say?

Well, at that time Morgan had a program of his own, and at one point—he's been talking about the faults of television—he looks right into the camera and says, "But you want to know what the real trouble is with television? You are."

Revisiting Catete

EMIR RODRIGUEZ MONEGAL

I can hardly recognize the old city: buildings like immense Art Deco chandeliers rise over platforms which overlook bridges jumping over crowded new avenues; a church like a monstrous cone of concrete; highspeed highways pushing Flamengo's shoreline into the Bay of Guanabara; and everybody talking (fast, excited) about the Metro, the new subway. And yet, I know these were the same streets Machado de Assis and his decent, elegant bourgeoisie used to haunt less than one hundred years ago. This is the same Catete, José da Costa Marcondes Ayres (the protagonist and narrator of Machado's last novel, *Counselor Ayres' Memorial*, 1908) used to long for so desperately in his diplomatic post overseas.

"A minha terra, o meu Catete, a minha lingua," exclaimed Ayres, returning to Rio for good after some thirty odd years. Yes, my land, my Catete, my language: because for Ayres (as for Machado himself), land, language and the old Rio neighborhood of Catete were one and the same thing. Today, Catete is upset by the subway work. In front of the Palace where Getulio Vargas reigned for so long, big deep trenches have been excavated, traffic is chaotic; dust replaces air. And yet, there is still some of the old Catete lying around if you know how to look for it. When I was in my early teens, I used to live there; first on the Avenida Beira Mar, later on Laranjeiras (the beauti-

ful street of the orange trees) and finally on Catete street. I attended the Lycée Français, in Laranjeiras, not too far from that Largo do Machado where I first saw the tallest palm trees of my life. The neighborhood was a bit rundown already, but I couldn't care less. It was heavy with the smell of coffee and those tropical fruits (mamão, abacaxi, all varieties of bananas) I used to love. And it was also full of the elegant, imaginary presence of Machado's characters.

I began to love them, then and there. They followed me around the Atlantic, south to Montevideo, north to England and France. Wherever I went, they seemed to fare well. Irony and reticence had prevented them from corruption. Machado's acute shyness had made them invulnerable to fashion and decay. I continued to pour over Braz Cubas' posthumous memoirs, over Quincas Borba (the character and the dog with his own name) and especially over my favorite, Dom Casmurro, who became his own (so deadly efficient) Iago. Naturally, I was too young to really enjoy the tricks Machado plays with narrative: tricks which some years later I would discover both in Sterne and Borges. But I was amused by his constant teasing of the reader, forcing him into a new awareness of his function as consumer of fiction. I was also too young to have read Machado's last two novels. In those days, critics did not pay much attention to them. *Epitaph of a Small Winner* (1881), *Philosopher or Dog?* (1891), *Dom Casmurro* (1899): those were the books to read. So, I read them and loved them, and Catete became haunted by Machado. Although half a century had already passed between his characters' experience of Catete and mine, I could not help feeling contemporary with them. Even today, I go back to Machado and rediscover my adolescence.

Only later I came upon *Esau and Jacob* (1904) and *Counselor Ayres' Memorial*. Machado was getting old when he wrote them. His beloved and so jealously guarded Portuguese wife would die the same year the first book was published: the *Memorial* was thus written in the saddest circumstances, and Machado died the year it was published. They are winter books: books where the novelist looks at life from an unbridgeable distance. In both, Machado invents an elegant, sixtyish spectator of life, Ayres, and through his sensibility presents two love stories. In *Esau and Jacob*, it is the love story of two twins who continue the fight begun in their mother's womb, becoming political rivals and suitors to the same innocent young heroine. Ayres looks at the conflict from a distance, takes notes in a diary (which is his *Memorial*), and very gently gives some advice which his friends are not in any position to follow. It is all very subdued, very Jamesian, except that Machado probably never read James, although he had read some of James' English and French masters.

In *Counselor Ayres' Memorial* (which chronologically overlaps part of the previous novel), the observer is also the protagonist, and the narrative consists of his diary for the years 1888-1889. But again, the protagonist is too remote and distant, even from his own affairs, to be more than an observer. Somehow the woman his sister wants him to marry drifts away and marries someone else. Ayres is left to record, with clear, ironic hand, the actions of others. His Brazilian name is symbolic: not Aries (the Greek god of battle) but *Aires*, a creature made of air, an Ariel. But Machado avoids leaning too heavily on allegory. He likes to suggest things. In *Epitaph*, the narrative is written from beyond this world by a dead man but no explanation is given about the technical details of the actual writing: what kind of pen, ink and paper he used: how he delivered the manuscript to the publisher, etc. In *Philosopher*, the man and the dog are doubles but there is no transmigration of souls, as there is in Bioy Casares' *Dormir al sol*. In *Dom Casmurro*, the protagonist is an Othello doubled with an Iago; he is more reticent and untrustworthy (all qualities indicated by his nickname of *casmurro*), but there is no attempt to explain him. To this day, Brazilian critics argue whether he was or was not cuckolded by his wife: a subject as passionately debated as the argument whether Hamlet was or was not Ophelia's lover. But in Machado's

last two books, allegory moves closer to the surface, especially in *Esau and Jacob*, where the story of the two fighting twins takes on the symmetry of *The Corsican Brothers*. In *Counselor Ayres' Memorial*, allegory runs deeper: Ayres' double is not another character, but his own text. Which brings us back to *Esau and Jacob*.

There is already a confrontation of two texts in that novel, although it is presented as a straight narrative, written (one can assume by the *Advertencia* at the begining of its text) by *Machado*. But the "author" was basing the story on the diary kept by Ayres: the diary which is quoted frequently in the text and which gives a curious perspective to the novel. Even Ayres' technique as diarist is discussed in the book (see Chapters XXXII, XLVI, XLIX, LIX, LXXXVI, C). The narrative and the diary work on two different levels much as Cortázar's in the third part of *Hopscotch*, where he uses the critical observations of Morelli to comment on the novel he was writing.

But the perspective becomes even more hallucinatory in *Counselor Ayres' Memorial*, because what we have here is *only* Ayres' text; no narrative by any "author" separates the reader from the text. And yet. The paradox is that the diary in itself establishes a distance. In writing about his own life, Ayres becomes two characters; the observer and the observed. The diary is no longer a transparent text: it also reflects the hand which is writing it. A few examples: on February 5, 1888, Ayres rereads what he has written the day before only to discover that it could have been shorter and more sober ("not so many tears," he says). On April 6, he warns the paper to take in all that his idle pen writes. On June 14, he admits that it would be easy to fill the pages with some "invention," something that didn't really happen. But on June 15, he comments on certain episodes, and warns the reader: "If this were a novel . . ." But it is not; it is a diary written by Ayres. On September 4, he insists: this is all prose, like the "possible reality" is.

Rimbaud already had discovered: "*Je est un autre.*" The moment one says "I," one becomes a character: "I." After Rimbaud, Jung and Yeats, Pound and Neruda rediscovered the value of the poetic *persona*: the mask the poet creates. In the *Memorial* the protagonist and the diarist are doubles. By taking notes on his life, Ayres becomes the "author" of his life; that is, a character. And what becomes of Machado?—because we know Ayres does not exist, and the *Memorial* is a novel and not the "possible reality." Machado, of course, writes both texts: Ayres' and his own. He is the "author": the one who watches while his character watches himself. But in making Ayres write his own diary (as he did previously with Braz Cubas' *Epitaph* and with Dom Casmurro's report), Machado creates a *mise-en-abîme*; he, Machado, watches Ayres watch-

ing himself. The *abîme* does not stop there because the reader watches Machado watching Ayres watching himself.

The whole question of what literature is about is found there.

I walk along Catete, enter Largo do Machado and follow Laranjeiras, watching for Machado watching for Ayres. The Rio of 1888 in which Ayres wrote his *Memorial* and the Rio of 1908 in which Machado rewrote it is the Rio of 1934 in which I first discovered Machado, and the Rio of 1975 in which I write now: characters becoming writers becoming readers in an endless and labyrinthine succession. The dust, the noise, the chaos of the future subway brings me back to a still unwritten but possible reality.

A Problematic Vision

JOSE GUILHERME MERQUIOR
Translated by Peter Lownds

JOSE GUILHERME MERQUIOR, the Brazilian critic and essayist, is the author of *Razão do Poema* (1965), *Arte e Sociedad em Marcuse, Adorno e Benjamin* (1969) and *A Astúcia de Mímese: Ensaios sobre Lírica* (1972).

The stories in *Papéis Avulsos* (Uncollected Papers) and the poems of the *Ocidentais* (Occidentals) give final shape to a problematic vision previously unknown to Brazilian literature and without parallel among other post-romantic writings. But the pessimism of Machado de Assis only had its impact when this problematic vision found expression in the "realistic" novel, the urban, contemporary novel; in other words, when *Epitaph of a Small Winner* was published. First published in the *Revista Brasileira* starting in March, 1880, *Epitaph* (which Machado, with failing eyesight, was forced to dictate to Carolina) did not appear in book form until the following year. The caustic flavor of the book clashed immediately with all the national examples of romantic idealization, while at the same time its bizarre humor and remarkably bold structure prevented any convincing identification with realistic or naturalistic models. The "author," that is, the deceased Braz Cubas, warns us at once that it is a "diffuse work," written "with the pen of Mirth and the ink of Melancholy." A diffuse work, full of digressions and extravagances, for in it, instead of the linear, objective narration of Flaubert or Zola, Machado adopted the "free form" of Laurence Sterne's *Tristram Shandy*.

This clue, furnished by Machado himself, has been followed to the letter by critics eager to characterize so strange a work in our fiction as *Epitaph:* a Sternian novel, composed in the wandering and capricious prose of a reader for whom Almeida Garrett's *Viagens na Minha Terra* (1846) (Voyages in My Native Land) possibly led to Xavier de Maistre's *Voyage Autour de ma Chambre* (1795) and this, in turn, to its own model—Sterne.

Still, at least two of the most obvious and important characteristics of *Epitaph* do not exist in Sterne. The first is the philosophical and sardonic nature of Machado's humor. This chilling irony, infected with "a certain peevish pessimism," as the departed author confesses, is very different from the eminently sentimental and congenial humor of *Tristram Shandy.* The acrid, bitter taste with which Machado's "Mirth" leaves us is completely absent from the amiable liqueur of Sterne; but the disturbing nature of Machado's humor derives precisely from its inquisitive, philosophical propensity, from its problematic vision. The second difference is the *fantastic* nature of the narrative. Sterne regurgitates eccentricities, but all of them are in the last analysis ascribable to the disordered perambulations of Tristram's spirit as he tells his autobiography; the author wanted to explore in his novel Locke's theory on the association of ideas: the key to psychic processes; thus the work is full of fantasy, but not the fantastic. Decidedly fantastic, however, is the narrative framework of *Epitaph,* starting with the fact that the novel has been written by a dead man, a radically posthumous "epitaph."

Here one might say that it is not right to take this supernatural air so seriously, for the fantastic is merely a humorous stratagem, a primary manifestation of Machado's sarcasm. No doubt, but it is precisely this fusion of philosophical and fantastic humor that allows us to discover the true genre of the novel: *Braz Cubas is a modern representative of the comic-fantastic genre.* The comic-fantastic genre, also known as Menippean satire, came into being in the West at the end of Antiquity; its most perfect realization is found in the prose satires of Lucian of Samosata (2nd century), author of the *Dialogues of the Dead.* The principal attributes of comic-fantastic literature, reformulated in recent times through Mikhail Bakhtin's studies of Rabelais and Dostoevski, are (a) the absence of any exalting perspective in the shaping of characters and their actions—an aspect by which comic-fantastic literature is clearly distinguishable from epics and tragedies; (b) the mixture of serious and comic which results in a humorous approach to the most crucial problems: the meaning of reality, the destiny of man, the nature of existence, etc.; (c) the absolute freedom of the text with respect to the dictates of verisimilitude; in the dialogues of Lucian, as well as in the novel of his contemporary, Apuleius (*The Golden Ass*), or in the work of Rabelais, the most hallucinating phantasmagorias are mingled simultaneously with purely veristic detail; (d) the frequency of the literary representation of aberrant psychic states: personality disintegrations, uncontrolled passions, deliriums (like the delirium of Braz Cubas); (e) the constant intermixing of genres—for example, of letters or stories—inserted in the global work (like the tales of Marcella, Dona Placida, Villaça and the mule driver in *Epitaph*).

We know by Machado's allusions that he knew and appreciated the works of Lucian —enormously popular in the Renaissance— as well as Lucian's baroque imitators such as Fontenelle (*Dialogues des Morts,* 1683) and Fénelon, or more modern ones like the great pessimist Leopardi (*Operetti Morali,* 1826). Certainly impressive are the analogies of conception and structure between the great expressions of the comic-fantastic genre and *Epitaph.* Lucian even has one of his characters, the philosopher Menippus, laugh boisterously in the afterlife, in a situation similar to that of Braz Cubas. It can be said that Machado elaborated a very original combination of Menippean elements, together with the "autobiographical" perspective of Sterne, and something of Maistre's. At the same time he accentuated the philosophical ingredients of one of the sources of *Tristram Shandy:* Montaigne's *Essays,* that classic of spiritual biography in an informal style. *Braz Cubas* is a case of the philosophical novel in a comic vein, a moralist's manual in merrymaker's rhythm. Instead of Sterne's humor via sentimental identification, what predominates in these pseudomemoirs is the spirit of parody, the satirical grimace, the profanity of Carnival. Almost no sentiment, no value, no conduct escapes this corrosive mockery. The official plot: the life of the rich *fainéant* Braz Cubas, with its loves, problems and ambitions, is only the point of departure for a moral critique expressed, in a profoundly artistic fashion, through narrative imagination and specifically motivated reflection, rather than through the abstract conceit or the isolated maxim. Therein lies the *raison d'être* of the novel's elastic structure: constant digressions (not always happy ones, in truth), the "snap of the fingers" given the reader; in sum: the humorous narrative technique of Machado de Assis.

The philsophical key to *Epitaph of a Small Winner* is naturally, the celebrated delirium of the author-character in Chapter VII. While dying, Braz Cubas hallucinates. He dreams that, mounted on a hippopotamus, he rides toward the "beginning of the ages" until a vast woman's figure, Nature or Pandora, lifting him by force to the top of a mountain, makes him contemplate the procession of the ages:

Just imagine, reader, a procession of all the ages, with all the human races, all the passions, the tumult of empires, the war of appetite against appetite and of hate against hate, the reciprocal destruction of human beings and their surroundings. This was the monstrous spectacle that I saw. The history of man and of the earth had thus an intensity that neither science nor the imagination could give it, for science is too slow and imagination too vague, whereas what I saw was the living condensation of history. To describe it one would have to make the lightning stand still. The ages moved along in a whirlwind, but nevertheless, because the eyes of delirium have a virtue of their own, I was able to distinguish everything that passed before me, afflictions and joys, glory and misery, and I saw love augmenting misery, and misery aggravating human debility. Along came voracious greed, fiery anger, drooling envy, and the hoe and the pen, both wet with sweat, and ambition, hunger, vanity, melancholy, affluence, love, and all of them were shaking man like a baby's rattle until they transformed him into something not unlike an old rag. They were the several forms of a single malady, which would attack now the viscera, now the psyche, and would dance eternally, in its harlequin trappings, around the human species. Pain would give way to indifference, which was a dreamless sleep, or to pleasure, which was a bastard pain. Then man, whipped and rebellious, ran beyond the fatality of things in pursuit of a nebulous and elusive figure made of patches—a patch of the intangible, another of the improbable, another of the invisible—all loosely sewn together with the needle of imagination; and this figure, nothing less than the chimera of happiness, either eluded them or let them hang on to its skirt, and man would hug the skirt to his breast, and then the figure would laugh in mockery and would disappear.

Upon seeing such misfortune, I could not repress a cry of anguish, which Nature, or Pandora, heard with neither protest nor ridicule; and—I do not know by what psychological law of inversion—it was I who began to laugh, with a laughter immoderate and idiotic.

"You are right," I said, "the thing is amusing and worth seeing; a bit monotonous, perhaps, but worth seeing. When Job cursed the day he had been born, it was for want of seeing the show from up here. All right, Pandora, open your belly and devour me; the thing is amusing, but devour me."

The march of the centuries is a "bitter" spectacle; man is a morass of passions, a useless rebel, for whom even pleasure is no more than a "bastard pain." Here we find again—with the *pathos* of bitterness—the vicious universe of "The Psychiatrist." Here it becomes very easy to understand the "peevish pessimism" of Machado's humor: his irony is, like that of Swift, clouded by a deep repugnance for the absurdity of the human condition. Nature, the "inimical mother," is a scourge; History, a catastrophe.

Between the biography of the hero and this tragicomic melody, Machado weaves a subtle counterpoint. Braz Cubas is a fool, a prisoner in his desires who aspires egotistically toward pleasure, power and glory. His story unfolds on a stage ruled by the degeneration of beings and experiences: the beauty of Marcella, his love for Virgilia, his tenderness toward his own sister—everything vanishes, everything rots. Not without purpose is the narrator's warning that the book "smells of the tomb." Destruction and cruelty are the norms of life. The hero, who kills butterflies, flies and ants with metaphysical voluptuousness, is not ignorant of the fact, like Gloucester in *King Lear,* that men are also flies in the eyes of the gods. Oppressed is no better than oppressor: as soon as he is freed, the slave Prudencio, once mistreated by the boy Braz, now whips his own servant without pity; Virgilia's domestics soon get even with her by spying on her adultery. The noblest causes always hide vulgar interests, for "who knows if at the foot of every great, public, conspicuous flag there aren't often various other modestly private flags, hoisted and floating in the shadow of the great one and which not a few times survive it?" Master of the unmasking, Machado is disciple of these French moralists for whom good sentiments are the hypocritical masks of egoism. As for social values, they are founded upon lies and conveniences. Braz Cubas' father adheres without pretense to the "stuffed shirt" theory ("Education of a Stuffed Shirt" in *The Psychiatrist and Other Stories*): "Notice that men," he says to his son, "are valuable in different ways, and that the surest way of all is to be valuable in the opinion of other men." Our very identity, our conscience, is a product of collective judgment: "to return to oneself" is "to return to others"—by way of the "stuffed shirt" theory we also return to the doctrine of the exterior soul.

From the social point of view, the bases of this dog's world are not difficult to circumscribe. The ambiance of Braz Cubas is that of the slaveholding elite of the eighteen-hundreds, in which indolence and sadism join hands daily. Astrojildo Pereira has shown Machado's sociological acuity, the fidelity with which he evokes the ways of life of bachelors and barons, mistresses and missies, servants and slaves. It is a communal space founded on the relationships of force, where the separation of the classes is only attenuated by a few cultural bonds

and rare political outlets; a social structure which reflects and stimulates the aggressive instincts. Nevertheless, the psychological ambiance most typical of this environment is not so much aggressiveness as tedium. Tedium, that "yellow flower, solitary and morbid," born in Europe, on the asphalt of industrial civilization, appears to have found an even better seedbed in our somnolent tropical Empire. The "voluptuousness of boredom" is an old friend of Braz Cubas. A good Schopenhauerian, Machado conceives of existence as a discouraging oscillation between pain and tedium. Perhaps only Baudelaire is comparable to him in the astuteness with which he defines the various tinctures of the moral spleen.

But all of this neurasthenia has a metaphysical source which is negativity, the destructiveness of time. Time, in *Epitaph,* is principally an agent of dissolution and decay; life is a continual putrefaction. Of the two faces of time—senescence and germination, aging and growth—Machado's pessimism favors the first. For him, the river of time leads to the sea of nullification, in the same way that the dying body of Braz Cubas was made "plant, and stone, and mud, and nothing at all." As in baroque pessimism, the supreme metamorphosis is under the sign of Nothing. And against this negative time only the intermittent sharpness of longing has power; only the most fleeting nostalgia for the past is capable of "shaking off all the miseries." Thus the hero, on his death bed, remembers with delight the years in which he loved the beautiful Virgilia. However, Machadian pessimism, which sees man as the plaything of (evil) instincts, is not similar to the rigid determinism of the naturalists. Liberty is an illusion but the determining factors are voluble and contradictory. Man "is a thinking erratum . . . each stage of life is an edition which corrects the one before it and which will be corrected also, until the definitive edition which the editor gives to the worms free of charge." Nature, reservoir of causes, matrix of evolution, is at times "an immense joke": she contradicts herself. Machadian pessimism does not acknowledge any logos: the world does not seem to him a cruel cosmos, but simply a chaos—a wretched chaos.

Machado de Assis did not adhere to any of the scientific credos of his time. However, he was profoundly influenced by the philosophy of Schopenhauer. According to Schopenhauer, the universe is Will, the blind, obscure, and irrational will to live. The law of what is real is no harmonious logos but rather a conflictive wanting, fatally wretched, insofar as it is necessarily unsatisfied. Because of this, pain, for Schopenhauer is the essence of things and only in the Buddhist ideal of renouncing desire can one attain any happiness. There is in *Epitaph* a character—Quincas Borba, the philosopher-beggar—who is presented as the creator of "humanitism." "Humanitism" is at the same time a caricature of the "religion of humanity" of the positivists (J. Mattoso Câmara) and a grotesque refutation of the "algesic" ontology—the ontology of pain —of Schopenhauer. Not that "humanitism" negates pain and evil; in the novel *Quincas Borba*, his motto will be the Darwinian "to the victor go the potatoes"—what it exposes in its own way is the full recognition of the agonizing, warlike quality of life. But Machado's irony is precisely in attributing to humanitism the arrogant pretension of justifying the rawness of reality, "explaining" all the disgraces of this world as just so many more victories for Humanitas, the highest principle of Being. . . . Like Voltaire's Pangloss, Quincas Borba is a ridiculous optimist. By turning "humanitism" into an absurd theodicy and its prophet into a grotesquely dogmatic figure, Machadian humor pays implicit homage to the metaphysics of Schopenhauer.

Moreover, the examples of Machado's other favorite thinkers tend to concur with Schopenhauer's pessimism. Pascal, Machado's master, had taught him to discern the kingdom of evil in the world. By radicalizing the Augustinian doctrine of the terrestrial world's corruption, the baroque Christianity of Pascal had revivified the gnostic idea of the intrinsic evil of the sublunar orb. In a philosophic chant, "Adam and Eve," Machado explicitly formulates the thesis that earthly reality is placed under the scepter of Satan; the majority of his characters are egotistical and evil, and their victims are worth little more than the delinquents. Biographical research has never ceased to indicate to what a degree this somber vision of existence mirrors the resentments of the sickly mulatto. In climbing the ladder of social prestige with rare vivacity, he still did not free himself from a sense of organic inferiority, from an ulcer "at the fountainhead of life" (A. Meyer)— an ulcer whose rancor would be transformed into affective impotence.

However, it is only hypothetically possible to attribute Machado's pessimism to his illness. More important than deliberating over the genesis of moral thought in an author is investigating his thought in the ambiguous but much more solid dominion of its exteriorization into a work of art and the relations of this work of art to the spiritual currents of its time. What is singular about the pessimism of Machado is its antagonistic position in relation to the Darwinism of the eighteen-hundreds, to the cult of progress and of science. Faced with the ingenuousness of scientism, which fancied itself the gravedigger of philosophy, the sarcasm of Braz Cubas reopens metaphysical interrogation, the radical perplexity in viewing the multiplicity of human nature. An artist like Machado de Assis took the blow that Darwin had struck against the anthropocentric illusions of humanity more seriously than the harbingers of scientistic evolution. Machado had learned from Montaigne not to forget how much man is an animal subject to nature and its whims, and not an invulnerable sovereign of creation, the arrogant master of his destiny. Only Quincas Borba overestimates man's place among the species—Braz Cubas prefers to ponder what "the hawks would say about us, had Buffon been born a hawk. . . ." Nature is indifferent to human consciousness. Thus no naturalism can subdue the acrid drama of Good and Evil, of pain and beatitude. No certainty, religious or scientific, subjugates Machadian pessimism. In Machado, the very spectacle of human madness is, at most, one perspective on the indecipherable enigma of the universe.

The humor of Machado de Assis is an

eminently philosophical *attitude*—but it is not a "philosophy." Metaphysically, Machado's humor does not have positive content. Herein, perhaps, lies his terrible freedom (which Graça Aranha intuited without comprehending), the audacious liberty that permits the comic-fantastic to border on the real. In this sense, the humorous structure of a book like *Epitaph of a Small Winner* is truly consubstantial with the Machadian vision of the world. Machado does not use humor to "illustrate" a philosophy: on the contrary—at times, by making a metaphysics out of the nonexistent—his humor *is* philosophy; and this phenomenon bestows a notable modernity on his work, for nothing is as modern as the eclipse of affirmative philosophy.

On the stylistic plane, this humor engenders the fictional experimentalism of Machado. An "experimentalism," it is understood, which has nothing to do with the "experimental" novel of the naturalists. On the contrary: by fictional experimentalism we mean exactly that free manipulation of narrative techniques which connects Machado de Assis to the great impressionist writers of fiction and sets him apart from the naturalists and their taste for the linear execution of narration. Along with his artistic prose, his keen perception of time and the "decadent" subjectivism of his characters (for example: Braz Cubas, Bento in *Dom Casmurro*, Flora in *Esau and Jacob* and Counselor Ayres in this last novel and in the *Memorial*), this is one of the elements which pleads most convincingly for the inclusion of Machado de Assis among impressionist narrators like Chekov, James or Proust. From a certain perspective, however, Machado seems even to go beyond impressionism. Impressionists like James or Proust attempted narrative techniques with intentions as realistic, as subordinate to the aims of verisimilitude as the linear, objectivist narration of Flaubert and Zola. Next to theirs, the Machadian narrative technique seems infinitely less serious, less compromised, more ludic. With Machado, the fictional experimentalism is animated by the spirit of mockery. His "cultured" references to classic mythology are typical: they always set a humorous perspective over the bourgeois reality. The apex of this ludic inclination resides perhaps in his very particular use of that characteristic of impressionist prose which is the phrase in a figurative style framed by a "realistic" narrative segment. Some examples gathered at random in *Epitaph*: zeugma (abstract + concrete): "Villaça bore in his eyes some sparks of wine and voluptuousness"; metaphor: "I went to see Virgilia; I forgot Quincas Borba quickly. Virgilia was the pillow of my spirit, a soft, warm, aromatic pillow, covered in chambray and Brussels lace"; mythological allusion: "I took her by the hands, pulled her gently to me and kissed her on the forehead with the delicacy of Zephyr and the gravity of Abraham"; prosopopeia: "But, half an hour later, when I left the ball, at four in the morning, what is it that I chanced to find in the depths of my carriage? My fifty years. There they were, the obstinate things, not numb with cold, not rheumatic—but snoring away their fatigue, a little covetous of bed and repose." And finally, this admirable portrait of Baroness X:

She never spoke much, or at length; she knew the subtle art of listening to others, spying on them; she would sit down in a chair, unsheathing a long, penetrating stare. The others, not aware of what was going on, would speak, gesticulate, while she alone was staring; now fixedly, now fleetingly, carrying her art as far as to stare at times into herself, letting her eyes close; but since her eyelashes were lattices, the stare continued its work still, ransacking the lives and souls of others.

Machado does not limit himself to lightly adorning narrative discourse: he takes obvious pleasure in developing adornments. In his work, the absence of "declamation" in dialogues and descriptions has its only parallel in the ostensible rhetoric of his language. Rhetorical, clearly, in the best, truest sense: conscious of the artificial and technical nature of the literary phrase. Machado, the "anti-tropical," abhors all emphasis with the possible exception of an emphasis of style. Nothing could be more erroneous than to think of him as a transparent narrator, a writer of fiction whose language is lost behind what is being narrated. To the most sensitive modern student of this work, Eugénio Gomes, goes the merit of having demonstrated the tendency of Machado's style toward figurative language and rhetorical relief. The Machadian phrase is, in fact, always affected: it demands that we look at it before we can see into it. But rhetorical style does not mean gratuitous ornamentation; there is no one less Parnassian, less verbose than Machado de Assis. Machado is a writer in whom the strongly rhetorical aspect of style, far from injuring, reinforces the mimetic energy of the language, its power to imitate, to effectively simulate (fictionalize) the concrete variety of life. And this too, more than a post-romantic trait, is something genuinely modern; something less akin to the impressionists than to a Joyce, a Borges or a Guimarães Rosa.

A New World Is Not a Home

ALEXANDER COLEMAN

There is a "different" feeling in the old American classics. It is the shifting over from
the old psyche to something new, a displacement. And displacements hurt . . .
it is a cut too. Cutting away the old emotions and consciousness. Don't ask what
is left.—D. H. Lawrence, *Studies in Classic American Literature*

Lawrence, although drawn to things Hispanic by spying primitive "dark gods" while wandering through New and Old Mexico, never paid much attention to Latin American letters. A bow to things Hispanic, maybe; but Brazilian? Forget it. Nonetheless, it's nice to talk for once with his help about American literature and American classics as if they were one, as if the literature were the psychic record of a single experience—the destruction of a classic, centuries-strong matrix, the creation of a new consciousness. This might be done as if linguistic barriers didn't exist between Spanish, French, Portuguese and English, as if every writer in the New World had burned his ships, snipped that long umbilical cord, "cut out," as it were, from what Lawrence so breezily calls the "old psyche."

What is an "old psyche"? Well, let us examine one—his name is Henry James; he is an American writer. Early in his career he recited, as the solidified Londoner that he most instinctively was, the "items of high civilization . . . which are absent from the texture of American life, until it should become a wonder to know what was left." What is missing? "Sovereign, court, personal loyalty, aristocracy, church, clergy, army, palaces, castles, manors, thatched cottages, ivied ruins, cathedrals, abbeys,

Oxford, Eton, Harrow, literature, novels, museums, sporting class, Epsom and Ascot." According to James in 1879, nothing more is missing from "the texture of American life." As Lawrence has already warned us in another connection, it's best not to ask "what is left." Or, as that master of American nothingness, Macedonio Fernández, stated many years ago, "so many people were absent (from a lecture) that, if one more didn't appear, there wouldn't have been any room for him!" This is one American way to fill up our lean and characterless space, be it a continent or a lecture room. Fill it by paradox, cosmic buffoonery, nihilism enough to outrage those Americans hanging on to the "old psyche" and send them packing back to their Lichtensteins of the imagination. This is one way of doing it, and it gave us Macedonio, Twain, Quiroga, Poe, Ives. Not bad.

Another way might be to consider all American literature of the 19th century as a vast effort of the imagination to create a liveable space with the means of language alone—to erect dynasties, townships, genealogies and whole counties out of the fabric of the word. "The repetition and persistence (of this myth) has been especially evident in American literature for the obvious reason that for the only time in history men could, with the prospects of a new continent, actually believe in their power at last to create an environment congenial to an ideal self." (Richard Poirier, A World Elsewhere, p. 7.) In effect, what we are talking about is the organization of the spatial imagination in American literature, of how coherence is gradually imposed upon what has no coherence, of how people make their new psychic homes where there was none before, and where Nature is variously a piranha, a snake, a bear, but never, never can it be construed as a garden.

Consider the case of Machado de Assis. Readers of the Epitaph of a Small Winner could hardly be aware that the author was a mulatto, severely stricken by a verbal block—stuttering—which rendered the most minimal communication impossible. He was known for his pained and painful silences, a good listener because he could do little

else in public. Nor could such an innocent reader trace his literary genealogy—the book seems like a bolt out of the blue in Latin American letters, even if we are sometime readers of Tristram Shandy. In other words, I'm trying to say that when we get there to Machado and his extraordinary novel, there is no there there, no psychic center, no axis, no sense of being, no sense of self, no surroundings, no furniture. Empty, empty, displaced. Part of the process of throwing out imported literary baggage lies, of course, in the structure of the novel, a burlesque Memoires d'outre Tombe written by the all-knowing seer that is Braz Cubas, dead as a matter of fact but still writing nonetheless. He is a displacement not only of what we think a writer is, but also of our common definitions of who is dead and who is alive, of what the living are able to do, and what the dead can seemingly do with the authorial omniscience such as Braz shows us from the other side of the River.

Much of this has to do with Machado's ominous view of the nature of Nature and the nature of Man. In contrast to what Leslie Fiedler calls "White Romanticism," which culminated, in a way, in Wordsworth's The Prelude, Machado partakes of a peculiarly Gothic yet still vacant view of Nature, American variants of which are on view with their own shadings in such works as The Narrative of A. Gordon Pym, Moby Dick, and The Scarlet Letter. I suggest that this vision of unfettered "sublime" Nature takes on terrifying resonances in America. "Who in this bowling alley bowled the sun?" asked Edward Taylor, a Puritan poet. Not surprisingly, it was Borges who first pointed out for Latin American readers this black and unremitting vision of Nature in Melville and Twain: ". . . The symbol of the Whale is less apt to suggest that the cosmos is evil than it is to imply its vastness, its inhumanity, its bestial or enigmatic stupidity." (Preface to "Bartleby the Scrivener.") On another occasion, Borges remarked upon Twain's ". . . conception of the stellar universe as a blundering perpetual machine, his continual creation of cynical or blasphemous apothegms, his vehement denial of free will, his affinity with the idea of suicide. . . ." ("A Vindication of Mark Twain," translation mine.)

Even taking into account a few Borgesian overlays in these statements, these passages may well be construed as a uniquely American vision of Nature, above all because of its absolute physical democracy—no hierarchies here, no "chains of being," no stratified "world pictures." Man and animal are unchained, Nature is a dramatic scene for countless pugnacious and striving egos. Is this "American," or is it, better still, a Darwinian vision which has finally found a home in the literary imagination of the New World? This may well be the answer—let us recall those imposing final sentences of the *Origin of Species,* where Darwin gives us the ultimate metaphor for his vision—"It is interesting to contemplate a tangled bank, clothed with many plants of many kinds, with birds singing on the bushes, with various insects flitting about, and with worms crawling through the damp earth, and to reflect that these elaborately constructed forms . . . have all been produced by laws acting around us. . . . Thus, from the war of nature, from famine and death, the most exalted object which we are capable of conceiving, namely, the production of higher animals, directly follows." (Darwin, *The Origin of Species,* Norton, p. 199.) As Stanley Edgar Hyman has commented on this passage, ". . . the Tangled Bank of Life is disordered, democratic, and subtly interdependent as well as competitive, essentially a modern vision." (Hyman, *The Tangled Bank,* p. 33.) It is a poetic vision of murderous ego and mindless victories of craft, cunning and strength. The "fittest" struggle, adapt and triumph. The "fittest" win by surviving the longest, and so do their species. What is interesting in all this is the various ways in which the late 19th-century literary imagination adapted an essentially biological and anthropological argument and laid it over man and his literature. Who are counted among the fittest among men? What is a "higher animal"? In the history of Social Darwinism in the United States, Andrew Carnegie and John D. Rockefeller took over the Darwin-Spen-

cer code to justify their killer instincts. And in literature, we are presented with a grim and humorless crew of authors. Whatever the virtues of Jack London or Frank Norris, it is clear that humor is not in line with the Darwinian vision they espoused. Quite the contrary, the code cast a Zolaesque pall over American letters for quite a few years. And the excesses were memorable and comic, but not in the way that the author intended. I recall a passage in a Frank Norris novel where a dentist pounces upon his anesthetized patient (female), driven on blindly by "the beast that had arisen within him."

Machado is a Darwinist in a way, but he is a unique case of a comic Darwinist in literature, an imagination which feeds of the wars and struggles of egos, atoms, bodies and Nations with an untoward glee, a writer whose character, Braz Cubas, begins his narration not only with a succinct description of his last moments, but also with a dedication of his story "to the worm which first gnawed away at the cold flesh of my cadaver." (This dedicatory is missing, by the way, from the otherwise faultless translation of William Grossman.) And indeed, it is the worm of time which sooner or later works away at everyone in the book, whether by disease or simple natural death. The other element, is of course, Braz's recognition of his own frigidity toward human warmth and love, the impulse of the "small winner" who knows that Nature cares not, that we weak humans sometimes do care, but that in the end it is best to imitate Nature to drive on headlong and upwards toward triumph, power and possession of beauty. To do otherwise would be not only to work against one's own interests, but worse, against what Nature expects of both man and beast, atoms and planets too.

The narrator, Braz Cubas, dead as he is, is given the opportunity for unique perspectives over the workings of Nature and the hapless humanity who strive and struggle to match "Mother's" implacability, froideur, and general disregard for individual destinies. What better way to view the tangled bank of men, animals and history than through Braz's geriatric delirium in Chapter 7, a regression to the not-so-beneficent source of all of us? ". . . An immense shape, the figure of a woman, then appeared before me . . . everything about this figure had the vastness of the primeval. . . . 'They call me Nature or Pandora. I am your mother and your enemy.' " Wishing Braz no other calamity than being alive, she lifts Braz into the air—he gets a close-up: "Its sole all-pervasive expression was that of eternal isolation, of changeless will, of the impassivity of complete egoism." As Stanley Edgar Hyman has said of Darwin's personification of the Goddess, ". . . She is not only omnipotent, she is omnipresent, 'daily and hourly scrutinizing, throughout the world, the slightest variations; rejecting those that are bad, preserving and adding up all that are good; silently and insensibly working.' She is also divinely impartial . . . 'a power represented by natural selection or the survival of the fittest, always intently watching.' She is no less a goddess." (Hyman, 39.)

Machado's version of "mother" Nature urges Braz to give up life in a burst of Epicurean pleadings. "Why do you want to live longer? To continue to devour and be devoured? Are you not sated with the show and the struggle?" Braz insists on the values of life itself lived to the end, but Nature seems to wish to accelerate his end by a final demonstration of the principle of the universe—"Yes, egoism; I have no other law. Egoism, self preservation. The tiger kills the lamb because the tiger's philosophy is that, above all, it must live, and if the lamb is tender so much the better; this is the universal law."

Images of the implacability of power, of devouring, of rapaciousness, are often present in the *Epitaph of a Small Winner,* on all planes of existence. Sometimes these images take on a grisly naturalism, such as the "horse" of Romanticism which finally lands up in the gutter, "where the realists found him, his flesh eaten away by sores and worms. . . ." Other instances come to mind —the image of the captain's dead wife, whose corpse is tossed off the boat which is carrying Braz to Lisbon. "The sea opened its belly, received the spoil, closed again—

there was a slight ripple—and the galleon went on." The same goes for the implacable way that death stalks Braz's mother and the old miser Viegas.

Only a Social Darwinist such as Braz could so breezily dismiss Eugenia; she is perhaps the only woman in the book capable of ameliorating Braz's power lusts, but she is dismissed for "eugenic" reasons— she is lame, she is unsuitable as a possible wife for a future minister, she must be thrown out. In the same way, Braz dispatches with the flick of a towel the black butterfly which not so mysteriously causes him unease; the butterfly must die because it is not blue, not perfect, just as Eugenia is packed off because she is lame. What counts is power and the possession of the world. No lame girls and certainly no black butterflies for Braz.

And so too for Quincas Borba's philosophy of Humanitism—what is this but a Darwinism unleashed onto society? "The hangman who executes the condemned may excite the indignation of poets, but in substance he is Humanity correcting in Humanity a breach of Humanity's law . . . envy is nothing but a fighting admiration and, as fighting or struggle is the greatest function of the human race, all bellicose feelings tend toward its welfare. From this it follows that envy is virtue."

So there *are* a few things we can say with certainty: that the book masks an anguished consciousness, that the "hurt" which Lawrence saw in the change of consciousness and the abandonment of the "old psyche" is something lurking just underneath the surface of so many American classics, and that Machado's vision of new American "feeling" and "space" is a rank and open confession that there is no home here, no bounded and protected spaces where man can let down his guard, where he can be what his apparent freedom so gaily invites him to be. This is my bleak reading of *Epitaph of a Small Winner.* I'm sorry, I don't think that it is quite the "classic comedy of ideas" that one reviewer called it many years ago.

Out-of-Print Masterpiece

Philosopher or Dog?
(Quincas Borba)

First published in 1891 as a sequel to
Epitaph of a Small Winner, *Philosopher or
Dog?* (Quincas Borba) *presents us with a
satirically pathetic precursor of the modern
anti-hero: Rubião. A miserable teacher
from the state of Minas Gerais, his sad lot
is suddenly transformed by a rich legacy
from the now defunct philosopher of*
Epitaph, *Quincas Borba, who also leaves
behind a dog of the same name, little
Quincas. Rubião, with his new charge as
well as his new fortune, sets out to climb
the social ladders in the Capital of the Empire, but is used materialistically by false
friends, manipulated in his adulterous play
with the worldly Sophia, and slowly
topples, on the brink of reification, into
destitution and madness. From a brilliant
work which deserves to come back into print
in the English translation of Clotilde Wilson,
the following selection combines bitter
recollection (for Machado, the mulatto, as
well as Rubião, his depersonalized protagonist) with sweet expectation in an ironic
interplay of race and class-ification.*

XLV

And while one weeps, another laughs. That
is the law of the world, my fine reader, and
it makes for universal perfection. All weep-
ing would be monotonous, all laughing,
tiresome. A good distribution of tears and
polkas, sobs and sarabands, finally brings
to the world's spirit the variety that it needs,
and the balance of life is contrived.

The one who is laughing at this moment
is Rubião's soul, with which he is going
down the hill, saying the most intimate
things to the stars, a sort of rhapsody composed in a language that has never been
alphabetized since it would be impossible
to find a sign to express its words. Down
below, the deserted streets seem to him to
be filled, the silence is a tumult, and feminine figures lean out from every window,
pretty faces and heavy eyebrows, just so
many Sophias that all merge into one single
Sophia. Sometimes Rubião thinks that he
has been rash, indiscreet. He recalls the garden episode, the young woman's resistance
and annoyance, and he is repentant. Then
he has chills, and he is terrified by the
thought that they may shut the door in his
face and cut off all relations, all just because
he precipitated events! Yes, he should have
waited; it was not the right occasion, what
with the guests, and lights everywhere; of
what had he been thinking, to have become
so indiscreetly, shamelessly amorous? He
thought that she had been right; she had
done well to send him away.

"I was crazy!" he said aloud.

He did not give a thought to the dinner,
which was sumptuous, nor to the wines,
which were generous, nor to the lighting,
which was such as is required by a roomful
of elegant ladies; he was thinking of himself, and he thought that he had been crazy,
utterly crazy.

But right after, the soul that had been ac-
cusing itself, defended itself. Sophia seemed
to have encouraged him to do what he did;
her frequent glances (finally she didn't take
her eyes off him), her courtesies, her singling
him out to sit beside her at the dinner table,
to be the sole recipient of her attentions,
her sweet murmuring of little pleasantries—

what was all this if not exhortations and solicitations? Then the good soul went on to explain the young woman's contradictory behavior in the garden; it was the first time that she had heard such words from anyone other than her husband, and, naturally, with everyone around, she must have been startled. Besides, he had been too effusive, he had rushed headlong without any gradual approach. He should have proceeded cautiously, and he should not have held her hands so tightly that he hurt her. In conclusion, he thought that he had been crude. The fear that they might shut the door in his face returned; but, then he went back once more to the consolation of hope, to an analysis of the young woman's actions and to her invention of Father Mendes, a falsehood of complicity. He thought, too, of her husband's esteem for him. And this made him tremble. Not only did her husband trust him completely, but he owed him a sum of money and three bills of exchange that Rubião had accepted for him.

"I can't, I mustn't," he kept saying to himself. "It's not right to go on. Of course, actually, I'm not the one who started it; she's the one who's been challenging me for a long time now. Well, let her challenge! I must resist! I lent the money almost without being asked for it, because he needed it very much and I was indebted him for kindnesses; it's true that he asked me to sign the bills of exchange, but he's never asked for anything else. I know he's honest and works hard; it's his confounded wife who's to blame, thrusting herself between us with her pretty eyes and that figure— Good Lord, what an admirable figure. It was divine today! When her arm brushed against mine at the table, in spite of my sleeve—

Thus, you see, all confused and uncertain, he was musing upon the loyalty he owed his friend, his conscience cleft in two, one part severely reprimanding the other, the other explaining itself, and both parts completely disoriented.

Finally he found himself in Constitution Square. He had been walking at random. He considered going to the theater, but it was late; so he went to São Francisco Square to get a tilbury for Botafogo. He

found three that came to him immediately, offering their services, each driver having particular praise for his horse, "a good horse"—"an excellent animal."

XLVI

The sound of the voices and of the vehicles awakened a beggar, who was asleep on the church steps. The poor fellow sat up, saw what it was, then lay down again, awake now, lying on his back, with his eyes staring up into the sky. The sky was staring at him, too, impassive as he, but without the beggar's wrinkles or his torn shoes or his rags; a bright, starry, tranquil, Olympian sky, just such a one as presided over Jacob's wedding and Lucretia's suicide. They continued staring at each other, the sky and the beggar, as if they were playing a sort of game to see which one of the two could, with sober face, outstare the other. They appeared to be vying with each other to maintain a quiet gravity, without arrogance, without humility, as though the beggar were saying to the sky, "After all, you're not going to fall on top of me," and the sky to the beggar, "nor are you going to climb up to me."

XLVII

Rubião was not a philosopher: the comparison that he made between his own anxieties and the ragamuffin's brought only a shade of envy to his heart. "That vagabond isn't thinking about anything," he said to himself, "he'll soon be asleep, while I—"

"Get in, sir. This is a good animal. We'll be there in fifteen minutes."

The other two drivers said the same thing in almost the exact words.

"Come over here, sir, and see—"

"Please, it's a thirteen-minute trip; we'll be there in thirteen minutes."

After some further hesitation, Rubião found himself in the nearest tilbury, and ordered it to set out for Botafogo. Then he recalled an old experience that he had long forgotten. It may have been without his being aware of it that the experience was now providing a solution to his problem. However it was, Rubião so guided his train of thought as to escape the immediate sensations of the evening.

It had happened many years ago, when he was very young and poor. One day, at eight o'clock in the morning he left his house on Cano (Sete de Setembro) Street, entered São Francisco de Paula Square and from there went down Ouvidor Street. He was somewhat worried, because he was staying at the house of a friend, who was beginning to treat him as though he were a three-day guest; and he had already been there four weeks. They say that three-day guests are putrid; corpses are long before that, at least in hot climates—. Well, our Rubião, simple as a good Mineiran, but suspicious as a Paulista, certainly was worried and decided that he must move from his friend's house as soon as possible. You may be sure that from the time he had left the house, entered São Francisco Square and gone down Ourives Street, he had neither seen nor heard anything.

At the corner of Ourives Street, he was stopped by a crowd and a strange procession. A man in judicial attire was reading aloud a sentence from a paper. Besides the judge, there were a priest, soldiers and idlers. But the chief figures were two Negroes. One of them, light-colored, thin, of medium height, kept his eyes lowered. His hands were tied behind his back and around his neck was wound a rope, the ends of which were fastened to the other Negro, a very black fellow who was looking straight ahead, confronting the crowd's curiosity bravely. After the paper had been read the procession continued on through Ourives Street; it had come from the jail and was going to Moura Square.

Rubião, naturally, was impressed. He spent a few minutes, as just now, in selecting a tilbury, as it were, with conflicting inner forces vying with one another in offering their horses; some suggesting that he turn back and go on to work, other suggesting that he go to see the Negro hanged. "It's so unusual to see a hanging. It'll be over in twenty minutes, sir."—"Oh, sir, let's attend to business." And our man shut his eyes and let himself be led by chance. Chance, instead of taking him down Ouvidor Street to Quitanda Street, deflected his route by way of Ourives Street, following the procession. He wouldn't see the execution, he thought; it was just to see the march of the culprit, the face of the executioner, the ceremonies — He didn't want to see the execution. Every little while the procession would stop, people would come to doors and windows, and the officer of the law would reread the sentence. Then the line would start up again as solemnly as before. The idlers who were hanging on kept recounting the crime to one another—a murder in Mata-porcos. The murderer was described as a brutal, ruthless fellow. Knowledge of the man's nature helped Rubião; it gave him strength to look into the face of the culprit without any feeling of faintness inspired by pity. However, it was no longer the face of a criminal; terror had concealed its depravity. Suddenly, without realizing how he got there, he found himself in the execution square. A number of people were there already; and together with those who were coming they formed a dense throng.

"Let's go back," he said to himself.

The condemned man had not mounted the gallows yet, and he would not be put to death immediately; there was still time to get away. And if he should stay, why not close his eyes as a certain Alypius did before the spectacle of the Circus? Note well that Rubião knew nothing about that ancient youth; not only did he not know that he had closed his eyes, but also he did not know that he had opened them right away again, slowly and curiously—.

Now the condemned man mounts the gallows. A shudder ran through the crowd. The executioner began his work. It was at this point that Rubião's right foot described an outward turn, in obedience to an impulse to go back; but the left foot, seized by a contrary impulse, stood still. They struggled for a few moments— "Look at my horse." "See what a fine animal." "Don't be cruel!" "Don't be timid!" And Rubião stood thus for a few seconds, just long enough for the fatal moment to arrive. All eyes were fixed upon the same point—his, too. Rubião did not know what creature was gnawing his vitals, nor what hands of iron were clutching his spirit, holding it there. The fatal instant was really just an instant; the culprit convulsively thrashed about with his legs, then he shrank together; and the executioner bestrode him gaily and with much skill. A great murmur ran through the multitude; Rubião uttered a cry, and saw nothing more.

XLVIII

"You must have seen, sir, that the little horse is good—"

Rubião opened half-shut eyes and saw that the driver was lightly shaking the tip of the lash to quicken the animal's pace. Inwardly, he was angry with the man for having evoked old memories. They were not pleasant, but they were old—old, and yes, they were healing, too; for they supplied a tonic that seemed to cure him completely of the present. So let the driver jolt him and wake him up. They were going up Lopa Street, and the horse was eating up the distance as if they were going down.

"You'd not believe what a friend of mine this horse is," continued the driver. "I could tell extraordinary tales. Some people say that I make them all up, but that's not so, sir. Who doesn't know that horses and dogs are the animals that are most fond of people? I think that a dog is even more so—."

The word "dog" made Rubião think of Quincas Borba, who, no doubt, was anxiously waiting for him at home. Rubião was not forgetting the condition stipulated by the will, and he had sworn to fulfill it to the letter. It must be said that along with Rubião's fear that the dog might run away went the apprehension that he might lose his inheritance. The lawyer's assurances made no difference. The letter had told him that, since there was no reversible clause in the will, even if the dog did run away, the property could not get out of his hands. Why did he care if he ran away? It would be better. He'd have less bother. Rubião accepted the explanation apparently, but he was still dubious. He knew what long lawsuits could mean, how judges often could not agree on a matter, what harm an envious or unfriendly person could do, and he dreaded (and this was really the substance of it all),

he dreaded being left without a penny. Hence, the great precautions he took to keep the dog in, and, hence, too, the remorse he felt for having spent the afternoon and evening without even once thinking of Quincas Borba.

"I'm an ingrate," he said to himself.

Then he corrected himself; he was more of an ingrate not to have thought of the other Quincas Borba, who had left him everything. Especially if, as it occurred to him, the two Quincas Borbas might now be one and the same, supposing that the dead man, less to purge his sins than to keep watch over the new master, had transferred his soul to the dog's body? It was a Negress from João d'El Rey who had suggested this idea of transmigration to him when he was a child. She said that the soul, full of sin, entered an animal's body; she even swore that she had known a notary who had become a *gambá*.

"Don't forget to tell me where the house is, sir," the driver said suddenly.

"Stop here."

XLIX

The dog barked from inside the grounds, but, as soon as Rubião entered, he received him joyfully, and no matter how annoying it may have been, Rubião made a great fuss over him. He was shivering at the thought that the testator might be present. Together the two went up the stone steps to the house, and stood for awhile at the top, under the light of the lamp that Rubião had asked to be left lighted. Rubião was more credulous than any sectarian; he had no reason to attack or defend anything, eternally virgin soil ready for any planting. From living in the capital, however, he had developed one peculiarity—among incredulous people, he was becoming incredulous.

He looked at the dog while he was waiting for the door to be opened. The dog looked at him, too, and in such a way that the deceased Quincas Borba seemed to be right there inside of him; the dog was looking with the same contemplative gaze with which the philosopher used to examine human affairs—. Another shiver, but Rubião's fear, though great, was not so great that it tied his hands. He spread them out over the animal's head, scratching his ears and his neck.

"Poor Quincas Borba! You like your master, don't you? Rubião's a very good friend of Quincas Borba."

And the dog slowly moved his head from left to right, helping to distribute the caresses to the two drooping ears. Then he lifted his tail so that his master would scratch underneath, and the master obeyed the dog's eyes, half-closed in delight, looking all the while like the philosopher's when he lay in bed, telling Rubião thinks of which he, Rubião, understood little or nothing. Rubião closed his own eyes. Then the door opened, and he left the dog outside, with as great a show of affection, though, as if he were letting him in. The Spanish servant took him down into the garden again.

"Don't strike him," Rubião admonished.

He did not strike him, but the descent itself was painful, and the friendly dog moaned in the garden for some time, Rubião went into the house, undressed, and went to bed. Ah! he had lived a day full of diverse and contrary sensations, from the morning's recollections to the lunch with his two friends until that most recent thought of transmigration. In between there had been the remembrance of the hanging and a declaration of love not accepted, yet scarcely rejected, guessed, perhaps, by others—. He mixed everything up; his mind bounced back and forth like a rubber ball in the hands of children. And, yet, the most important sensation was that of love. Rubião was astounded at himself, and he was repentant. His repentance, however, was the work of his conscience; whereas his imagination would not relinquish the lovely Sophia's figure at any price—. One o'clock, two o'clock, three o'clock— Elusive sleep— Where had the three hours gone? Half-past three— At last, after all this thinking, sleep appeared, squeezed the classical poppies, and, after that, it was just a moment. Rubião was asleep before four.

Machado de Assis in English

Epitaph of a Small Winner
Translated by William L. Grossman. Noonday Press, 1952 (Paper).

Dom Casmurro
Translated by Helen Caldwell. Univ. of California Press, 1953 (Cloth).

Philosopher or Dog?
Translated by Clotilde Wilson. Noonday Press, 1954 (Cloth) O.P.

The Psychiatrist and other Stories
Translated by William L. Grossman and Helen Caldwell.
University of California Press, 1963 (Paper).

Esau and Jacob
Translated by Helen Caldwell, Univ. of California Press, 1966 (Cloth).

The Hand and the Glove
Translated by Albert I. Bagby, Jr. The Univ. Press of Kentucky, 1970 (Cloth).

Counselor Ayres' Memorial
Translated by Helen Caldwell. University of California Press, 1972 (Cloth).

Pro or Contra in Casmurro

WILSON MARTINS
Translated by Peter Lownds

Almost every reader of *Dom Casmurro* has been tempted, at one time or another, to prolong the novel well beyond the confines of the last chapter by debating the innocence or guilt of Capitú. Ultimately of course, the question is an idle one, because it is not Capitú's "real life" which matters but rather adultery in the context of the novel itself. Yet no one seems to have noticed in the midst of so much discussion that Machado de Assis himself had at one time passed his own judgment on the problem—a judgment against Capitú or, if you will, against the kind of existential entanglement in which she, as well as her husband Bentinho, unwillingly participate. And when I say "at one time," I am not referring to a moment around 1899, when the work was published, nor to any moment in the work itself. I am speaking rather of *The Hand & the Glove*, which had appeared in 1874 and whose "differences in composition and manner" from his later works Machado would attribute, in 1907, to the "thirty-some years elapsed" between its first appearance and its subsequent reprinting.

In 1874, however, Machado had already called the reader's attention to the fact that his principal, if not exclusive, interest in writing *The Hand & the Glove* had been the composition of its characters, notably Guio-

WILSON MARTINS, Professor of Portuguese at New York University, has just finished his six-volume study *Historia da Inteligência Brazileira.* His collected critical writings, *Punto de Vista,* will be published later this year.

mar: "the action serving only as a screen," he had noted with revealing insistence, "on which I cast the outlines of their profiles." Not even he knew, nor could anyone know at the time, that Guiomar was actually a first draft of Capitú and that *The Hand & the Glove* was a preliminary version of the more successful *Dom Casmurro;* just as *Dom Casmurro,* a quarter of a century later, would tell the story of another Guiomar (that is, Capitú), who by staying with her own Estêvão (now called Bentinho) fails to find her Luis Alves. Or who finds him, actually—but too late and in the wrong circumstances—in Escobar, her husband's closest friend.

The evidence which points to *The Hand & the Glove* as a tentative version of the famous story of Bentinho is impressive. To begin with, observe that the entanglement in the two novels is exactly the same. (The *entanglement,* but not the circumstances, since *The Hand & the Glove* is a *Dom Casmurro* with no need for adultery.) The implicated characters also correspond perfectly: Guiomar with Capitú, Luis Alves with Escobar and Estêvão with Bentinho, in complete symmetry. Even the secondary characters seem to parallel one another: thus, for example, the part of the slippery dependent within the structure of *The Hand & the Glove* is played by Mrs. Oswald while it is reserved for José Dias in *Dom Casmurro.* The drama of *Dom Casmurro* therefore results from the fact that the Capitú (the "hand") was never destined for Bentinho (the "glove"). In fact, everything might have been different had the *glove*-Escobar auspiciously encountered the *hand*-Capitú. Then probably the *glove*-Sancha (Escobar's wife) fit, at the right moment, its intended *hand*-Bentinho. In *Esau and Jacob* Machado proposes an even more complex plan for the dialectical play of these same personality non-encounters—this time with twins.

In one of the didactic commentaries with which he so often delighted himself—not merely a skeptic, Machado was a Professor of Skepticism—he took the opportunity to delineate precisely the "moral" of *The Hand and the Glove,* thus setting forth, *a contrario sensu,* the moral of *Dom Casmurro:*

Destiny shouldn't have lied nor did it lie to Luis Alves' ambition. Guiomar was right: here was a strong man. A month after their marriage, as they were talking about those things newlyweds talk about, namely themselves, and recalling the brief period of courtship, Guiomar confessed to her husband that on that occasion, she had recognized in him all the power of his will.

"I saw that you were a man with a resolute mind," said the girl to Luis Alves who, seated, was listening to her.

"Resolute and ambitious," added Luis Alves, smiling. "You must have perceived that I am one and the other as well."

"Ambition is no defect."

"On the contrary, it is a virtue. I feel that I have it and that I am sure to make it succeed. I am not counting only on my youth and moral strength: I am depending on you also; you will be a new source of strength to me."

"Oh, I hope so!" exclaimed Guiomar.

And in a mischievous manner, she continued: "But what will you give me in return? a seat in the Chamber of Deputies? a position as minister?"

"The prestige of my name," he answered.

Guiomar, who was standing before him, her hands locked in his, let herself slide slowly down upon her husband's knees, and the two ambitions exchanged an affectionate kiss. Both settled down as if that glove had been made for that hand.

The lesson is clear but let us beware of reading it too quickly. *The Hand & the Glove* is not simply a "novel of ambition" and is in no way Stendhalian. It is a love story in peculiarly *Machadian* terms, that is to say, one in which love is merely the by-product of a whole cluster of factors. Machado writes about the passion of love, to be sure, but only as a passion conditioned by still other passions stronger than itself. In this sense two virile temperaments like Luis Alves and Escobar are bound to impress corresponding temperaments like Guiomar and Capitú; but two feminine temperaments like Bentinho and Estêvão would never be able to awaken similar passions (admiration and respect) in the souls of those same women, whom they both meet at the wrong time. Guiomar and Capitú are like birds of prey—terrifying carnivores; Estêvão and Bentinho, on the other hand,

are pallid vegetarians—cooing, defenseless doves.

Machado effects one of the most compelling examples of his non-encounters in the case of Escobar's wife, Sancha. She is a sketchy character at best and appears briefly, yet who can now fail to see in a different light the *only* episode in *Dom Casmurro* which at first glance seems gratuitous and unnecessary: the fleeting encounter in Chapter 118—appropriately entitled, "The Hand of Sancha"—between two searching spirits, the clasp of two understanding hands. Anxious and trembling, they seek the respective gloves that might fit them:

Sancha raised her head and looked at me with so much joy that because she was such a friend of Capitú I would have liked to kiss her on the forehead. And yet Sancha's eyes did not ask for fraternal expansiveness—they seemed sultry and imperious, they said something quite different, and soon she moved away from the window, where I remained looking pensively toward the sea. The night was clear.

From my corner, I sought Sancha's eyes, near the piano: mine met hers on the way. They stood still, and remained facing each other, one pair waiting for the other to pass, but neither passed, just as happens on a narrow path when two stubborn travelers meet. Caution drew us apart. . . .

As we were leaving, my eyes spoke once more to the mistress of the house. Her hand pressed mine, and lingered there longer than usual. . . .

I still felt Sancha's fingers pressing mine, and mine hers. It was an instant of madness and sin. It passed quickly, and when I held Time's watch to my ear, I heard only the minutes of virtue ticking away.

Structurally, the scene takes place while the same clock which punctuates these moments of passion has already begun its slow movement toward Escobar's moment of dying. It is the chapter in which the characters are already addressing themselves with foreboding to the raging sea in which Sancha's husband will take his fatal exercise. Clearly, none of the participants is aware of what is going to happen but the possibilities inherent in their impending trip to Europe, where the occasions for adultery will be real enough. The announcement of the voyage, the suspenseful contact of eyes and hands, and even a premonition of the tragedy all take place within the context of a violent sea breaking upon the nearby shore—that same surf which, by definition, has been the very image of the eyes of Capitú, whose tears on the following day will be for Bentinho the first clear sign of his disgrace.

Through the symbolism of the sea, Machado de Assis seems to suggest not merely the stereotype of "bottomless passions," but, above all, the sea's aspect of natural, impersonal force. In *Dom Casmurro*, the sea is presented fundamentally in the form of a tide as destructive and consuming as the passions. As a means of communication and a threshold to happiness, the sea appears in its tranquil and beautiful dimensions in only two episodes: Bentinho's frustrated trip to Europe and the later project of a common voyage. From a structural point of view. Chapter 118 is the focal point of the novel where Machado draws together Escobar's idea of the promise of a voyage, the premonition of his death, the virtual adultery of Sancha, the tumult of passion assaulting Sancha and Bentinho, the stormy sea heard throughout the night, and, finally, the "statue of the Commander" (a barrier which, unlike its Tirsonian counterpart one cannot but imagine already removed or removable), in the classic shape of a picture on the wall:

The picture of Escobar, that I kept there, alongside the one of my mother, spoke to me as if it were he *in propria persona*. I struggled sincerely against the impulses I had brought from Flamengo: I cast from me the image of my friend's wife, and called myself disloyal. Besides, who could say there had been any intention of that sort in her goodbye gesture and in the previous ones? . . . Even if there had been some sexual intent, how could I be sure it was anything more than a swift flash of sensation, destined to die with night and sleep?

Hence, relations between Bentinho and Sancha escape being adulterous only because, in a seeming paradox, the marriage in question is terminated on the following

morning when Escobar drowns. His corpse will separate Bentinho from Sancha, as well as from Capitú, just as surely as the living man brought them together in the first place. In the Machadian ethic, the actual adultery of Escobar and Capitú has the same value as the consummated marriage of Guiomar to Luis Alves. And the emotional adultery of Bentinho and Sancha is exactly proportionate to the failed marriage of Guiomar and Estêvão.

And just as Bentinho lacks the courage to kill Escobar (a solution presented retrospectively in the mirrorlike episode of Bentinho's failure to poison his own son—and Escobar's look-alike— Exequiel), so Estêvão lacks the courage to kill himself (symmetrically enough) in the sea, as "a kind of final vengeance he would take upon those who were making him suffer so much, complicating their happiness with remorse." Nor does Estêvão have the courage to kill Luis Alves. He and Bentinho have been reduced in the end to bitter impotence and complete anonymity:

[Estêvão] instead of diving into the water and into nothingness as he had planned, returned sadly home, stumbling like a drunkard, leaving there behind him his entire youth, because what he was taking with him was something discolored and dry, sterile and dead. The years went by, and as they moved along, Estêvão sank into the vast and dark sea of the anonymous masses. The name which didn't pass from the memory of his friends died right there, when fate took him away from them. . . .

Likewise, Bento Santiago finally loses even his own name and is transformed into Dom Casmurro, "a closed and hidden man," an accidental and ironic appellation which he deems, however, significant enough to supply the title of the story, symbolically summing up his life. Both Estêvão and Bentinho end up vegetating "in some corner of the capital." Their weakness has allowed them to be crushed by the strong: by Guiomar and Capitú. It seems that Humanitism more than the deliriously Darwinian philosophical system of Quincas Borba is in many ways a pure reflection—a skeptical reflection—of the mind of Machado. ◯

The Second-Best Horseman of the Apocalypse

English Version by Thomas Colchie

CORRESPONDENCE

Friend Casmurro, I propose to enrich (as inconspicuously as possible), by means of a new technique, the halting and rudimentary art of reading: this new technique is one of deliberate anachronism and erroneous attribution, whose applications are infinite. This technique prompts us to go through the *Odyssey* as if it were posterior to the *Aeneid* and the book *Los naipes del tahur* by J. L. Borges as if it were by J. L. Borges. This technique fills the most obscure mind with wonder.

Pierre Menard to Dom Casmurro,
Nîmes, 1904

My Dear Menard, I, in turn, offer you the following suggestion by way of dramatic reform: that the drama begin with the end. Simple enough! In that way, for example, your Othello would kill himself and Desdemona in the first act; the next three acts should therefore be given over to the slow decrescent action of jealousy; and then you close with the initial scenes of the threat of the Turks, the explanations of Othello and Desdemona, and the shrewd admonition of honest Iago: "Were I the Moor, I would certainly not be Iago." As for *Los naipes del tahur*, let me tell you that I have not and never shall give credence to such works.

Dom Casmurro to Pierre Menard,
Engenho Novo, 1904

PROLOGUE

I am not talking of "influences," a horrible
professional word clung to desperately by
those who can not find the true keys. . . .
                                            Cortázar

He defers to Poe, Mallarmé and Leon Bloy,
refers to De Quincey,—his mask of stunned
erudition, "to conjure up whole pages of
Livy"—prefers, from time to time, Schopenhauer for coming "nearer the truth than the
vague remedies of hope in a future life."
These writers, and others, are juxtaposed
in a single, rather slim volume of slightly
peculiar *pseudo*—at times, "fictional"—essays of extraordinary power. A few critics
are surprised, for some reason, to discover
in his work the elements of a new genre.
Perhaps I should say are *confused* enough to
discover, for the *reader* has no "genre,"
and to encourage him to pursue "a work of
art . . . for what it allows *him* [that is, the
reader] *to bestow upon it*," is not, necessarily, to invent something new. I would
rather see it as a form of collaboration, an
appeal to the symmetrically minded, even
if, in fact, it is a hopeless penchant for the
anachronistic, since, after all, the writer is,
in reality, condemned to the past, and the
reader, irrevocably, somewhere in the future. Equally compelling, although slightly
more pathetic, is the periodic obsession for
"the fascinating problem of writing a novel
concentrated in a few sentences and yet
comprising the cohobated juice of the hun-
dreds of pages always taken up in describ-
ing the setting, drawing the characters, and
piling up useful observations and incidental
details."

In effect he postulates the hieroglyphic
concerns of some of his precursors:

The words chosen for a work of this sort
would be so unalterable that they would take
the place of all the others; every adjective
would be cited with such ingenuity and finality
that it could never be legally evicted, and
would open up such wide vistas that the reader
could muse on its meaning, at once precise and
multiple, for weeks on end, and also ascertain
the present, reconstruct the past, and divine

the future of the characters in the light of this
one epithet.

Still, to demonstrate the source of an idea
is one thing, whereas to encompass his particular use of any idea is quite another.
Therefore, let me just limit my preface, for
the time being, to the following declaration: it is without exaggeration the strangest
book I have ever read.

A. Borges by Machado?

Je est un autre.
                                            Rimbaud

All books somehow remind me of *Los naipes
del tahur* (The Cards of the Sharper), a
small and, for the moment, out-of-print
work bearing the modest imprint of one
J. L. Borges. Have you not heard of it, Reader? I am not surprised. You have? I am interested . . . That you have not read it I
am certain. I would not be astonished if
the work, like Herbert Quain's, has not had
a hundred readers, nor fifty, nor even ten.
Five? Possibly four. After all, how many
have read the blank verses of the *Panegyric
of Saint Monica*? Its author? But the case
speaks for itself. Perhaps four readers, if
one counts the publisher, the librarian and
the author himself. But there are readers so
obtuse that they understand nothing unless
you tell them everything: "Everything—and
what's left over!", in the words of J. M.
Machado, that mild-mannered disciple of
this same Borges, *avant la lettre*.

In an Autobiographical Essay dated August 12th, 1970, Buenos Aires, Borges refers contemptuously to a book of "bitter and
relentless" literary essays, *The Sharper's
Cards*, which he had composed in Spain
and destroyed before returning to Argentina
in March of 1921. Yet, Rodríguez Monegal
claims to possess a photograph, dated 1936,
of Bioy Casares and Borges actually tear-
ing the manuscript in half, playfully, but
with the title page still visibly intact—it contains a black and white lithograph of a
winking queen of spades, bearing the signature of Nora Borges. The existence of the
manuscript was finally confirmed by a "Post-
script" to *The Aleph*, dated March 1st, 1943,

where Borges confesses painfully to having submitted to a jury for the National Literary Prize a manuscript entitled *The Sharper's Cards* or *The Cards of the Cardsharp*—I cannot remember. I do know that the manuscript was returned immediately, because it apparently contained some political essays with veiled references to "daggers," "harlots," and "the low flight of organized vultures." Through the kind offices of my friend, Carlos Frías, of Emecé, and the Miguel Cané Branch of the Municipal Library in southwestern Buenos Aires, I have in front of me, on library loan, the third chapter of a 1947 revision of *Los naipes del tahur,* the chapter entitled—I can only wonder why– "The Second Best Horseman of the Apocalypse."

Why the third chapter, Reader? I still entertain at least some hope of modestly winning the public's favor. I am neither morose, nor tight-lipped, nor withdrawn to myself. I am a *Cubas,* you might say. And I have already taken a First, tentative step in the right direction "by avoiding a long and detailed Prologue," as Cubas himself might have suggested, "even to the point of obscurity." Notice, now, if it please you, Gentle Reader, with what grace and with what poise I take my Second step, perhaps the most dangerous step of them all. Others would devote a whole chapter to it and call it their "Transition." I prefer to save paper. Look: I have already mentioned a certain J. M. Machado, whose mentor was none other than this same softspoken Borges with whom we have concerned ourselves so exclusively, perhaps unwisely, up until now. Would it surprise you to discover that Borges' disciple, and not the master himself, is the subject of my monograph? Prepare for a shock, Gentle Reader, and prepare for my Transition: the third chapter of *The Cards of the Cardsharp* is devoted, entirely, to J. M. Machado. Shall I lend you my trapeze, available for the service of difficult transitions and useful for the handling of abstract concepts? And notice how I have saved you the trouble of reading the first two chapters: one, frankly, of a fantastic nature, and the other entitled "Footnotes to *Father Brown.*"

2.

I am beginning to be sorry I ever undertook to pen this monograph. It ambles, despite all efforts to the contrary—yours *and* mine. Dear Reader. Perhaps if we were to call upon the First, the Third and the Fourth Horseman to lead us directly to "The Second Best Horseman of the Apocalypse," perhaps then . . . But the trouble is, are we certain that Second Best and Second Horseman are one and the same? Might we not be underestimating? I think it best, even Second best, to turn directly to the third chapter of *The Cards of the Cardsharp,* which begins: "Of all my precursors—I have counted only fourteen, while others, somewhat unjustifiably, prolong this number— none was ever so presumptuously and yet so rigorously Borgesian as J. M. Machado. Is it superfluous to advise the reader against the existence of not a few, previous, although imperfect, Machados? To insist that I refer to neither one of several Spanish Machados, nor to the Brazilian Romantic novelist and poet, Maria Machado—later called Maria de Assis, until finally, more recently, perhaps a little too perfectly, Machado Assis? Is there not rather a kind of infinitely persuasive, plagiarizing Machado who, like some Cortázar or some better Borges, a Des Esseintes or De Quincey, inexplicably pleases and, at the same time, disturbs me so? The purpose of this essay is to explore the indices of my reckless emotion."

Reckless? Ridiculous. There seems to be some mistake here. I spoke clearly of a *disciple,* not a "precursor." Yet the seventeenth paragraph forestalls any objection: "I have not unreasonably drawn attention to the fact that J. M. Machado was one of my more exacting precursors. I have yet to indicate, however, the radical nature of his undertaking. He was ever entertaining the implausible. His posthumous memoirs, for example,—*Epitaph of a Small Winner*—are impeccably complete, consummately posthumous." Borges had already admitted by paragraph twelve: "For a time I was obsessed with nothing less than what Machado called his 'extraordinary method'—he refused to divulge his formula, but continually applied it to the composition of those nearly perfect memoirs, '. . . written here in the world beyond.' I surrendered myself to several hundred pages of self-inflicted torpor. Eventually, I set them aside, but not before I had managed to borrow from his seventh chapter, 'The Delirium,' my story of 'The Secret Miracle,' as well as 'The South,' which he seems to have considered, politely, to be my best work. I do not know which one of us has written some of those pages." No, I have not misled you. The hoax, Dear Reader, is not in. . . . It has to do with reality, which is beginning to yield on more than one account. The truth is, it was itching to yield. Come along: the tale is quickly told, even twice. Otherwise, good riddance!

B. Machado by Borges.

> The work of a man already dead.
> Braz Cubas

I wish to qualify now, if not to vindicate, my provisional skepticism concerning a Brazilian novelist and his tradition. If I succeed, in some small way I shall have repostulated a once sublime axiom: the Equivalence of Windows. Gentle Reader, *Gentle Reader*, no need for panic nor flying trapezes! "No three-legged cats here," as my friend Cubas would have reiterated, brandishing his havana. Just open the window. Open the window! That one is stuck? Too much paint, probably. Well then, open another: they are all the same. They cannot all be so difficult to raise. Perhaps now, with a little air. . . . But you want something concrete. Perhaps a mistaken identity? All right, here is your Mistaken Identity.

J. M. Machado simply does not exist. Nor Maria Machado, for that matter; nor, manifestly, Machado de Assis. They are all Borges—"*Borges par lui-même*," as Rodríguez Monegal once wrote to me, I think, from Paris. They are all nothing more than the equivalence of windows. There, now! What, still not satisfied? Then I might just as well give you the snap of my fingers— but I have no wish, Gentle Reader, to prolong your Melancholy. Instead, I will give

you a plaster: a Cubas plaster, to be precise. Here is the plaster.

In his Commentaries to *The Aleph and Other Stories*, dated November of 1970, New York, Borges wearily confesses: "My story deals in its own way with the problems of immortality. I have for so many years lived with the fear of never dying." Elsewhere, in *Dreamtigers*, he had complained: "I who have been so many men, uselessly, want to be no one anymore," and again, elsewhere, "I have been Homer; shortly I shall be everyone else." I doubt that he was in fact Homer, but I have no reason not to believe he was J. K. Huysmans, Herbert Quain, Joseph Cartaphilus, or De Quincey. He was also, unequivocally, Cervantes and Caesar, Lima Barreto and Emma Zunz, the minataur, Cortázar, you—Gentle Reader—, Quevedo and Dr. Brody. He was J. M. Machado.

To document my provisional skepticism for the purposes of this monograph, we have only to return to 1824, when in Memphis (State of Tennessee), Borges was still the aging cartographer George Buckley—a detective, freeloader and scoundrel in the slave trade. But the tide was soon to turn against Buckley and his business. In 1838, he got wind of a secret society—the Phoenix, it was called—, signed conventicles and promised a disciple. The same year he sailed to Rio, was taken for a mulatto and, unwilling to trust in apprentices, impersonated himself, this time with the name J. M. Machado de Assis. His guiding purpose, although it was impractical, was not unthinkable: he wanted to obliterate himself. In 1858 he was a proofreader, two years later a reporter. In 1879 a brilliant career in the Ministry of Agriculture was interrupted by sudden septicemia. While he convalesced, his wife Carolina read to him works by Sterne and La Bruyère, who together reminded him of someone he could not remember. His recovery was considerably more painful to him than the illness itself, and he began to have nightmares, epilepsy and an absorbing obsession with the *Summa Theologica*. He was inflicted with a minute sensation that he was only partially himself. It was in this condition that he wrote his *Epitaph*—"a Utopian Memoir," he called it, because the narrator himself was dead throughout his confession. A pipe dream only, for in the darker sequel, *Philosopher or Dog?*, a similar protagonist is abjectly humiliated by his own reincarnation. In 1900, Machado published *Dom Casmurro*. In the fifty-sixth chapter, he refers to himself for the first time as Luiz Borges. Elsewhere, as Machado, he confides: "O ancient streets! O ancient houses! O ancient legs!" It was, after all, the turn of the century, and Borges must have felt a familiarly cyclical and periodic urge, not unlike our Spring in the North, but I can only surmise. I do know that, in 1908, as Jorge Borges, he published, in a Buenos Aires daily, a refreshing translation into Spanish of Oscar Wilde's "The Happy Prince." The same daily brought a stunned world news of Machado's death from Brazil. France declared a national day of mourning. Borges had grown weary from the composition of vast books. "A better course of procedure," he suggests in the 1914 "Prologue" to *The Sharper's Cards,* "is to remember that these books already exist, and to avoid writing altogether." In that same work—may I take the trouble to admonish you, Gentle Reader—he had deftly managed to turn himself, a *disciple,* into his own *precursor:* that "infinitely persuasive and plagiarizing" one who had caused us both so much Melancholy, once upon a time. Still, Jorge Luis Borges was without a profession. He felt inept, indolent and suffered from insomnia. Geneva was too isolated; Spain was patently anachronistic. He preferred, aside from minor hoaxes, to write little more than occasional footnotes. And nothing was more insipid, more insufferable than his own mind—than those footnotes to himself. In 1938, after two or three fitful periods of despondent uninventiveness, he capitulated once again, contracted septicemia, asked his mother to read to him in English and French, and began to work on an abbreviated version of the *Epitaph,* which, pitiably, morbidly—perhaps sarcastically—he would entitle "The South," —in order, I can almost hear him say, to differentiate the eternal glaciers of my previous "Delirium," where everything was so white with snow, from the present suburb

of hell. Here I conclude, Gentle Reader, the personal part of my monograph. The rest, if it is not on the tip of your nose, at least adheres to the floating sensibilities of the public at large. I have played my last trick, as it were, and have only to return you to the Sharper and *his* Cards:

I believe I once referred to the radical nature of his undertaking to precurse me. I believe I also disappointed him in this respect. Machado would often berate me, while we sipped mate together with Macedonio: "And still, and still, you have not written a novel." He also complained that I had reduced the *baroque* to "a four-letter word, when in any other language it contained at least six letters." He said that while one of his characters had been obsessed with no less than 500 *contos,* I had contented myself with an ordinary Uruguayan coin worth 20 *centavos;* and that while Braz Cubas was out witnessing the universe from atop a hippopotamus, I preferred to sleep in the cellar. He accused me of *reductio ab adjectivo.*

Still I was able to learn a great deal from the master. I may have been a better poet, but as a writer of fictions no one surpassed him. Even Macedonio could barely preface him. His masterpiece was, unquestionably, *Dom Casmurro* and, looking back on it now, I believe I have never strayed beyond that book. My story of "The Waiting" is parasitical by comparison. Essentially they have little in common: in my version, a man without a name flees an assassin or zealot named Villari, assumes the identity of his assassin, has a toothache, goes

to the movies, until—awakened to his own execution—he finally manages to get some sleep. Much more imaginatively *Dom Casmurro* relates the story of a man named Santiago, who tries to escape something altogether more ambiguous and perplexing: his own jealousy; later, he assumes his own identity—now as Bento, now as Casmurro—and finally, exhausted by life, he takes to rebuilding the house of his childhood, that patient labyrinth of walls which he hopes will trace the image of a face, a mirror:

The house in which I live is *mine*. I had it built specially, to satisfy a desire that is so personal I am ashamed to print it,—but here goes. One day a number of years ago, I decided to reproduce in Engenho Novo, the house in which I grew up on old Rua de Matacavallos. It was to have the same appearance and plan as the other house, which had disappeared. My purpose was to tie together the two ends of my life, to restore adolescence in old age. Well, sir, I did not succeed in putting back together what had been nor what I had been. If the face is the same, the expression is different. If it were only the others that were missing, no matter—but I myself am missing and this lack is essential.

Villari, of course, was caught in a similar "act of magic," when the blast obliterated him, and brought my story to its own abrupt finish.

Superficially, though, I am embarrassed to demonstrate just how much the two works have in common. The address of the hotel, for example, number 4004, I took from a lottery ticket in a dream that figures prominently in *Casmurro*. The lottery system itself also plays a part in at least one of my more interesting failures. Neither one of us, I might add, was ever troubled by the innocence or guilt of our protagonists: "The text must suffice in itself, if it pleases you, Excellent Reader," Cubas once admonished, examining his fingernails, "or if it does not!"

Other refinements I managed to apply more propitiously to some of my later tales, especially "The Aleph" and "The Zahir." No conspicuous reader of Chapter 55 in *Dom Casmurro*—which contains the first and last verses of a sonnet the author "never wrote"—will fail to detect the combinatory model for my collaborative games like "Pierre Menard, Author of Quixote." And it was Machado who virtually invented that peculiar form of oxymoronic structure he would eventually name the "Art of Eternal Interimities." Normally,

oxymoronic structure applies to a word an epithet which seems to contradict the word in question, such as the Dark Light of the Rosicrucians, but in the hands of Machado it was something more akin to the Universe itself. Thus, in *Dom Casmurro*, when his son, Ezekiel, arrives from Europe with news of Capitú's untimely passing, and laments, "She was beautiful, my mother, in death," Casmurro's response can only be: "Breakfast!"

J. M. Machado died on March 29th, at 9:02 in the morning. Beside him were a *Panegyric to Saint Monica* and this brief note, scratched in pencil:

I saw the Albuquerque brothers for example, I saw Bastos and his skinny legs, I saw you, Luiz Borges. . . . How many other faces stare up at me from the cold pages of the *Panegyric*.

Footnote to the Prologue

Consta de *cuatro* letras: $J(K + L + M)$!
Baruj Spinoza

There is no exposition on the art of symbolism that does not mention *A Rebours* (Against Nature), the *uncanny* biography of a *fin-du-siècle* ascetic, who was thoroughly versed in the works of Mallarmé and who did much to "predicate, at least in a rudimentary way, the satanic splendors of Thomas de Quincey and Poe, of Charles Baudelaire and J. K. Huysmans." Although Borges fails to mention him in "About William Beckford's *Vathek*,"[1] his words are curiously applicable to certain pages of the above essay, but not all of them.[2] ⬤

---

1. Or the fact that, like Villari, he was also "once afflicted in the middle of the night with an abominable toothache."

2. Translator's note: the "Prologue" employs texts from J. K. Huysmans' *Against Nature*, Penguin Edition. The remaining texts are basically derived and adapted freely from Machado de Assis' *Dom Casmurro* and *The Psychiatrist and Other Stories*, University of California Press, *Epitaph of a Small Winner*, Farrar Strauss and Giroux, and all the works by Borges in English translations. I have never read *Los naipes del tahur* (The Cards of the Sharper).

Genesis of the Clowns

WILSON HARRIS

An excerpt from the Guyanese novelist's latest work, to be published this spring in England.

(Frank Wellington was a government surveyor in British Guiana, South America, in the 1940s. He emigrated to Britain in 1950 and because of a crucial letter he receives in the 1970s is drawn back to analyse profoundly his relationship to the members of the survey party whom he led into the coastland Abary river and into the interior Cuyuni river of Guiana.

The members of the crew come from different ethnic and cultural backgrounds and Wellington visualises their coming to the paytable to receive their wages as they used to do on survey expeditions. Their wages change into a symbolic currency now through which he weighs up afresh patterns of "frozen genesis" in the encounter between Atlantic cultures and heartland cultures of South America.

In the following excerpt it is Reddy, an Amerindian, whose people had lived for centuries in the deep interior above the tidal rivers and whose pole of the sun-god relates to constantly falling waters symptomatic of an anchored earth, who comes to the paytable.

Frank Wellington begins to glimpse the implications of a Copernican wilderness in the marriage of static "animistic" cultures to an Atlantic "science-based" culture. He begins to sense in the labour Reddy gives and in the wage he receives, a deeper currency of fear and heroism, comedy and self-sacrifice, bound up with new menaces and with the new substitute father-figure he (Wellington) becomes as his instruments begin to replace the pole of the sun-god.

Implicit in the Copernican wilderness is an unfathomable (rather than static) centre around which cultures revolve. Wellington glimpses this as the complex theme of objective and subjective freedom. He glimpses also the price heterogeneous societies pay to achieve this in apparent catastrophe or transition towards a medium of consciousness susceptible to dual insight and creativity and to original compassion.)

The sun rolls across the paytable into another head of day and night and Reddy's turn to receive his pay has come around. As he advances to the paytable I consult the loom of light into which I threaded my inquiries about him, his background, his gods, his people, in 1942.

Counter-revolving currencies of light is the cash he receives now—in which I would like to pay him now—thirty-two years after the Cuyuni expedition, twenty-six years after the Abary.

I do not know if he still sees me after all this time as a medium of light, a substitute father-figure into which he projects his fears of a stranger universe I chart on my maps as I project into him my tides of a familiar ocean, familiar to me but which he encounters with the greatest trepidation.

A misconception is joined between us which has endured for centuries as the frozen genesis of an encounter between the Atlantic moon and the polar sun of the Equator.

Reddy's antecedents are clowns of light.

He and his brothers are the walking shadow of the gods who once ruled the Guiana highlands.

It is a token of their fall that they became members of my expedition into the Cuyuni river when I surveyed it in 1942.

On the completion of that survey at the end of the year he wished to remain with me and travel down from Bartica to the coast. I consented and so it was in 1948 that he came into the Abary with me where he witnessed something that confirmed what he had seen before with awe, with terror, namely, objects that moved of their own accord against the stream. . . .

It was a mere sixty-five miles from Bartica to the coast—a day's journey by river steamer—but it constituted a great divide for him he had never crossed before. He had feared it too much.

It has taken me a long time to sort out his pay—to make it appropriate to the wonders and great fears and curiosities he entertained as a member of my crew when he subsisted upon, spiritually subsisted upon, the joint seed of the moon and the sun. . . .

It falls on the paytable now—the cash I endeavoured to give him—with a faint sound like the spray of a wave that touches one's lips and I am as conscious of Hope's scars as of Frederick's lined ships on the breast of the sea. . . .

Reddy's ancient gods, whose shadow he projected into me at the paytable as medium of his fall, were born into a world of eternally descending waters that fell from the mountains and illumined the land.

I say "illumined the land" advisedly for falling water was to them an instinctive guarantee of light, dark as it seemed to me when I ventured into the interior in search of hydro-electric power.

It was a darkness into which I groped as into the mother of the gods upon a pole of sun driven into the Guiana highlands as the origin of a female earth.

Thus began Reddy's substitution of me into a father-figure which was threaded—little though he knew it—into my own childhood upon a watershed I demarcated on a map, a watershed he demarcated in his legends as substantial with the pole of the sun from which all rivers fell.

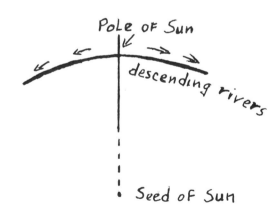

My first error of misconception in sorting out Reddy's cash in 1942 and 1948 was to devalue the currencies of light built into his fears. His was a heroism I failed to understand, a submission to terrors money alone could never assuage. Perhaps at this late stage of time I may be able—I say it again—(but who knows?) to assess all that it meant to him to become a member of a crew which seemed to him the embodiment of motivations that shook the very ground under his feet.

I misunderstood the spirit of the tides as they addressed him. I misunderstood the spirit of the ground on which he trod. Indeed the notion of the "tides"—of non-tidal flow as of tidal flow bound together—was alien to Reddy's light of the gods.

He saw his rivers descending from the pole of the sun, a function of the sun, the extensive seed of the sun planted in mother earth. He saw how I appeared to possess that pole in my instruments and, therefore, alien as I was to him in my assessment of the waters as tides (a non-tidal flow and tidal flow "mathematically" bound together) he had no alternative but to see in me the masked god of light from olden times returning to address him now, in almost unimaginable terms, across the paytable.

Take first of all the element of "mathematically bound tides".

It was at Bartica that three rivers sacred to Reddy—the Essequibo, the Mazaruni and the Cuyuni—crossed and met.

For me it was a technical banality that the three rivers had fallen beneath the plane of the sea and were subject now for the first time, in their long falling career degree by degree out of the highlands, to Atlantic tidal influences.

For Reddy it was a phenomenon, a great terror, to witness logs and trees moving of their own accord in unison with heretical tides against the falls. For not only was it a phenomenon of objects but of the very stream itself, the very water itself, that moved contrary to the shadow of the gods to support objects right into the falls that were ready, therefore, to run of their own volition uphill.

All waters seeded to the sun moved forever down (and this was the experience of the folk in the highlands for centuries) and it signified a labour of love he understood—payment in coin or kind—when the folk built paddles with which to manipulate their vessels upstream back home, since they needed to return from places they visited downstream, before they came to the end of a falling world. But no labour was possible that turned the waters against themselves except a quarrel amongst the gods, a quarrel between the sun and the moon in which the earth was fatefully involved.

As though the extensive seed of the sun came into counter-revolution with the dutiful seed of the moon far out in a bottomless river at the end of the world north of Bartica where the three rivers crossed; a bottomless river indeed that became susceptible now to returning upon itself like an intuition of mother earth (veiled by the sliced moon) actually revolving around a stationary sun. But how could the earth itself move up hill like a log against the stream of the sun?

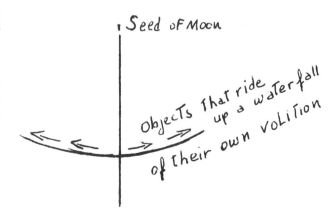

Perhaps the time had come, which Reddy feared most in his legends, when a woman would lie upon a man and ride up hill into a fall as into the divided seed of the moon. . . .

He wondered about his own sister now who had come with them to Bartica and whose appearance seemed to her brothers curiously corrupted, dangerously altered against the suspension of the paytable in a bottomless stream. For the first time Reddy felt he possessed no medium of exchange, in coin or kind, to understand the inroads of the conception of a stranger universe . . . except through instruments such as I possessed . . . or through the purchase of a gun as huntsman of game or the purchase of an elaborate rod as fisherman of fish. It was a way of emulating the gods, the quarrel of the moon and the sun imprinted on earth.

I became a government surveyor at the age of twenty-four in 1942 and led my first expedition into the Cuyuni river. I remember the year with enormous clarity of the sun in one's ribs, the thirst for adventure, the malaise of youth. I had applied to join the Royal Air Force which had a recruiting office in Georgetown. I had more than the necessary mathematics training as a cadastral surveyor but failed the medical test because of "deep-chested asthma" as it was called.

The interior Cuyuni and the coastal Abary are alien bodies indeed, one multi-layered, erosive, accretive cycle, sometimes breathless savannah, the other a secret labyrinth of Breath/Bush, and yet an instinctive thread runs through them like a winding involuntary garment it is difficult but necessary across the years to begin to unravel.

One could call it an instinctive thread indeed as curious as the light feather with which I invested Moseley in a marketplace of giant brides gliding through space. . . .

Reddy's diminutive stature embodied that pilot thread again.

He was scarcely more than five feet two inches tall. A beaked, parrot-like nose and a sudden disconcerting way of laughing lips, laughing sometimes it seemed to me at nothing at all. I did not know whether those lips laughed because they thought others wanted them to, or whether a hidden congenial spring lay there. I did not *see* Reddy's awe, Reddy's fear which suppressed itself with each sudden flare of gaiety, bark, laugh. Yet I was conditioned myself. And the more I studied (without appearing to study) his brand of heroism—the more it rose over the years into unconscious bits and pieces within other conscious lives, other conscious selves planted in the paytable—the more I wondered about the very essence of comedy itself.

I designed some curious headlines and printed them into my field book.

MYSTERIOUS CONTAGION AFFECTS VISIBLE AND INVISIBLE SELVES IN THE MIRRORED HEAD OF GOD UPON WHICH ALL COMEDY SUBSISTS.

"Think," I wrote into the paytable, "of the chorus I acquire when I become a universal laugh-maker built into the sun. My slightest breath is threaded into that chorus, the timing of an eyelid, the purse of my lips, the angelic bond I sport with devils. All are instinctive money-chorus as the globe itself rings with laughter.

"And what is remarkable perhaps is the ribald sensation that grows irresistibly into one's facial muscles because of intensities of predictable response in the built-in chorus that affects the laugh-making machines of the universe. As though each machine enjoys laughing at itself laughing, its laughter is the surest equation of tragedy, suppressed tragedy, native tragedy that possesses no theatre of its own and, therefore, hooks itself into every comic (cosmic?) display of talent as a cover-up of universal terror."

In ways like these—as I looked deeply into the arts of the paytable—I became acquainted with Reddy's immersion in a void as relating to the sun, relating to antecedents of light. For the comedy of the sun was the tragedy of polarised cultures on the brink of an awareness of themselves as satellite never sovereign. It was a huge Copernican step, an unimaginable step, for economic man, for primitive man, for economic child, primitive child, to take. . . .

And implicit in the Copernican wilderness is an unfathomable (rather than static) centre around which cultures revolve. I glimpse this as the complex theme of objective and subjective freedom. I glimpse also the price heterogenous societies pay to achieve this in apparent catastrophe or transition towards a medium of consciousness susceptible to dual insight and creativity and to original compassion.

And so in reflecting upon a medium of exchange, reflecting upon the cash I sought to pay him, I was astonished at his (and my) built-in apparatus for self-deception, for self-distancing ourselves from ourselves that bordered upon nevertheless an irony of consciousness, a humility of consciousness of a new earth. . . . And this made as baffling as ever the currencies of light in which we traded. . . . As it made as compulsive as ever the masks of light to which we were drawn out of fearful relationship, out of a desire for a new beginning. . . .

I needed a fortnight at least to order stores, hire riverboats, appoint rivercaptains, make all sorts of arrangements, before we set out from Bartica.

I had not yet recruited my full crew and came upon Reddy for the first time one afternoon skirting Sorrow Hill. Sorrow Hill stands like a huge barrow made by nature at the junction of rivers and converted by man into the burial place of nameless rivercaptains and forgotten crews.

I was ascending the hill towards him, his three brothers and his sister all moving in single file with unselfconscious stealth like breathless bodies on a trail in the Bush.

I was to observe this, again and again, in the months to come, when Reddy and his brothers worked for me in the heart of the interior, this immaculate stealth grounded in reflexive concentration like creatures equipped to slide along a stream, to walk upon water, upon a hill of water that brought them, as they brought it, into a conversion of bone and land, conversion of the drowned.

Was it a curious internal femininity, the masculine feminine of light craft and plural bodies, plural waters, light disembodied

chorus, comedy of the sun? And as the thought crossed my mind I was aware of the gun in Reddy's hand that flashed in the arts of the paytable in my head and protruded like a silver tooth in a grinning box of earth.

I was gripped by the angled sensation of coming death, of having been glimpsed, when I least bargained for it, by an eye in the mouth of a gun.

Reddy himself had not really seen me and to this I pinned a certain hope.

Yet it seemed clear beyond the shadow of a smile, in the light of aimless death, implacable feud, that was happening everywhere, that the gun moved of its own volition on the hill, it floated, it turned, it was wholly indifferent, it took aim, it was pointing at me.

I felt myself on the edge of an everyday tragic precipice, already devoid of breath, already killed. And I wondered what would happen if it fired. Would I be seen for what I was—a head myself among clowns? Would I hear its bark, the bark of sound into silence as I fell? Would that be the end of my built-in chorus, the death of offstage chorus that prompted my facial muscles to smile, or would I be re-born unblinking, open-eyed, into a new germinating stillness or vision of noise?

Would I perceive the divisions of the moon in the flash of Reddy's sister's skin, her bright yellow dress and her ripe skin on Sorrow Hill?

There was a strange corruptibility in her that I welcomed with open arms since it bargained equally for coming life as for the coming of death.

It was the corruptibility of every labour of love in which the gift of lips, breasts, arms, thighs, by Reddy's sister's body to me was subject to the lie of the paytable, the greed of the paytable. A gift that sprang from the instinctive gift of life itself in all times and yet was susceptible to misunderstanding, was susceptible to a slumbrous passion and deed of cruel appetite in its very gratuitousness, its very self-defencelessness that seemed too forward to be true —too generous to be innocent—so that it encompassed one like a burning explosion in one's flesh . . . capital flesh. . . .

All at once Reddy's file itself was here, borne close to me by the hill. He had seen me now. The muzzle of his gun was pointing elsewhere. It had turned away toward innocuous childlike horizons that constellated themselves upon it. Reddy laughed and said as if the gun spoke to me now, its substitute father—

"Mr. Wellington sir I hear you need a crew. Hope, your foreman, send me. Me and my brothers know the Cuyuni river well."

I felt abnormal, irrational, relief. (A month ago I had read in a local paper a man had been shot here on this very hill by a jealous lover. There was a woman whose life had been spared.) I was alive. I am alive. Perhaps it is all an illusion that one is alive when others are dead. Is it an illusion to be fathomlessly alive, to bark, to laugh, to sing? I cast aside my shadowy past-knowledge, I cast aside my shadowy fore-knowledge. A jumble of voices out of past unconsciousness, ever-present consciousness, speak. They arise out of Sorrow Hill as out of blackened rooms under a glaring sun when the ice-man passes and moistens one's parched lips. (A penny for an iced soft drink at Frederick's Bartica shop.) Reddy says the foreman of my party whose name is Hope has sent him. I look at Reddy's sister and seek to relate her to other women's arms around other men's lives (it is a way to pull oneself up and back into the land of the living) and to the self-creative, self-destructive, fire in the child-gun's secret comedy, secret genesis of fatherland and motherland by which all men are masked, rewarded, afflicted. . . .

Surrealism and Leonora Carrington

ANNA BALAKIAN

Surrealism was a global attitude beyond the dimensions of esthetics, a way of life, a way of comprehending life and its contingencies: *"Je chante la lumière unique de la coincidence"* said André Breton, the leader of the movement. It was a way of relating one life to another, and the human with the other entities of the biosphere. It was aimed at a restructured vision that embraced the universe as a continuum: *"ta chair arrosée de l'envol de mille oiseaux de paradis / Est une haute flamme couchée dans la neige,"* said Breton as he fused the flesh of the woman he loved with birds of paradise and flame burning in the snow. The continuum placed each man and woman in an unbroken relationship, holding a thread of the magnificent tapestry of the composite whole.

That was the essential dream but social conventions had corrupted the power to dream, to imagine, to be free. In the first page of his First Manifesto, Breton stated the case of the human condition as no longer tenable: "Man, that incorrigible dreamer each day more discontent with his fate." He deplored the loss of childhood and yearned for a new golden age that might restore the pristine unity of the world where the sensual and spiritual world fuse again as they were in the beginning into a single experience and where reality would

ANNA BALAKIAN is Professor of French and Comparative Literature at New York University and is the author of *André Breton: Magus of Surrealism,* currently being translated into Spanish. She read this paper at a symposium on Leonora Carrington during a retrospective showing of the artist's work in the Center for Inter-American Relation's Gallery.

encompass the imaginary, and all dichotomies disappear.

In the terms of André Breton's definition of surrealism there were certain basic theories to which its disciples would adhere. But as surrealism manifested itself in literature and art all over the world, contrary to other such movements, it did not develop a standard style. Each writer and artist associated with it preserved his own originality and for each surrealism was—as it was for that heroine of Breton's biographical prose, Nadja—the blue wind that passed in the trees.

In his Second Manifesto Breton described his disenchantment with the political side of the effort to transform the world and declared that henceforth surrealism must proceed toward deep occultation: *"Je demande l'occultation profonde du surréalisme."* He evoked the names of Nicolas Flamel, Hermes, Abraham le Juif, and other alchemists of medieval and Renaissance times.

It is in this occult direction of surrealism that Leonora Carrington and most of the Latin American surrealists proceed in their art, whether in painting or writing. Therefore, the fact that Leonora Carrington has chosen to make Mexico her home is one of those marvelous coincidences that Breton ever sought in the universe of man.

I see in Leonora Carrington's painting two remarkable qualities that are in the surrealist spirit: the monistic unity which involves man, animals, the vegetable and the mineral worlds, and the alchemistic power with which she transgresses our surface realities and conjures phantom figures that seem to

Bird Pong, 1949. Egg tempera on panel, 45x72.5 cms. Collection of Edward Frank Willis James Esq.

derive not from superspheres but from within, from the substrata of human consciousness, what Paul Eluard called once *"Les Dessous d'une vie ou la Pyramide Humaine."* The phantoms inhabit one creature after another, creating transparences around them wherever they are lodged.

Among the most salient processes distinguishable in art works—including those of Leonora Carrington—that have emerged under the auspices of surrealism during the last fifty years are the following:

1. *A process of dehumanization.* This is the first manifestation which owes as much to Dada attitudes and the influence of Duchamp as to surrealism: we could say that in the case of Carrington the dehumanization is not in the direction of reducing the human form to lines and object forms. In her case the dehumanization occurs when humans assume animal forms: there emerges a whole menagerie that reminds one of

medieval fables but the embodiments are not those of congealed moral characters as they were in the fable but rather those of ambivalent impulses and desires.

2. *The juxtaposition of distant realities,* which has had wide notoriety as a surrealist process. I do not have to enumerate the number of such frighteningly remote entities that participate in the composition of Leonora Carrington's paintings. What is particularly successful in the case of her juxtapositions is the absence of artificial and sensation-seeking elements so often present in the works of other surrealists. One realizes as one gazes upon these juxtapositions that they are not arbitrary at all but have subterranean links between them, revealing what must be in the personality of the artist: eruptive conflicting forces, dichotomies that find peace with each other only when they locate their eternal positions on the canvas.

3. *The mingling of human, animal, vegetable and mineral kingdoms.* Max Ernst is particularly adept in this type of execution as for example in that well-known painting on his called *"L'Oeil du silence."* But whereas Ernst's paintings of this nature make for static silences, Carrington's suggest dynamic cataclysms.

4. *The hallucinatory quality,* placing one image or object into another—of course the most publicized element of surrealist writing and painting. Dali is particularly well known for this form of pictorial metaphor and calls it *paranoia critique.* Many of Breton's verbal metaphors also employ this process rather than that of juxtaposing distant realities; his remarkable love poem, *"L'Union libre"* is indeed based on the poet's power to situate the elements of the beauty of his loved one within various manifestations of the natural world. Placing one into another was also the basic activity of the ancient alchemist: it is the basis for transformation and metamorphosis—both products of the philosopher's stone, which in the case of the surrealists, becomes either the pen or the brush. Notice how magnificently Leonora Carrington achieves one image within another in her canvases; for example, in *Viper, Viper of the Sea* or in the one called *Le Roi Dagobert,* where the head of hair, becomes, in our vision of it, the trunk of a tree. In Latin American surrealist poetry it is particularly the image of the Mandrágora that suggests this amalgamation.

5. *The dislocation of the function of the living or of the inert*—a marvelous example of this in Carrington can be seen in *"The Bird Pong."*

6. *The ability to create new forms and entities*—the most evolved form of surrealist manifestation over and above the ones previously mentioned. This final and most creative state of surrealism is achieved by Miró and Yves Tanguy, and often by Leonora Carrington as well. But whereas the creations of Miró and Tanguy have a stylization which gives our universe a reductively pure and tragically insensitive character, Leonora Carrington's visions have turbulent movement, colors that betray the intensity of fire and ice, and ferocious animistic forces that seem ready to burst out of their canvas barriers.

The projection of the dream into reality, which was a principal surrealist aspiration, presumed the artist's capacity to dream fertile dreams although theoretical surrealism tended to put more emphasis on the ability to project the dream than on the capacity itself to dream.

The animal embodiments of fear, desire, rebellion, escape that emerge from Leonora Carrington's dreams or nightmares give the viewer not only the visions themselves but a marvelous sense of the force of conjuration which resides in her.

Attempts will be made by art historians in years to come to identify the images which through repetition tend to become symbolic and typological in her works. Some will be attributed no doubt to cabalistic emblems, others to aboriginal Aztec symbols, as well as to Greek myths such as the Minotaur present in so much of her work.

But beyond the identifications, what is more important is the way she uses the pristine alphabet of man's collective imagination. Her personal imprint transcends coterie surrealism as well as cabalistic stereotypes. She elaborates her own mythology, which has remained consistent in her work through the years. Her colors may change, her painting media may differ from time to time, but the vision has an unflinching and ever recognizable signature that places her among the top artists who were touched by surrealism.

André Breton said: *"L'oeil existe à l'état sauvage."* The eye is primitive and savage in Leonora Carrington's world but beyond that, there is a striking use of the eye. It seems to have an independent existence of its own, free of the rest of the organs, looking fiercely out of some dark pit, dragging the inner vision into the outside world. The piercing look that fixes upon the viewer seems to be the result not of something terrifying gazed upon in the outer world but of a reaction to some gut experience within. And sometimes where the eye should be there is some other thing taking over the visionary role and casting a spell on the viewer. In this connection, consider, for instance, *The Ancestor* (1958), *the Candle Game* (1966) and *Lepideptera* (1969).

Finally, perhaps the greatest contribution of surrealism to contemporary civilization has been the extension of the definition of poet so that it can apply to any artist—or even to nonartists, like most of us—who recognizes the blue wind passing through the trees. In the case of painters, surrealism separates the repetitive technician from the truly creative one. Mind you, I do not agree with those who characterize Leonora Carrington as a spontaneous artist. She is a superb technician, her work delicately wrought, even when designing indelicate things! Her art is geometrically conceived and constructed with architectural premeditation, unlike certain others who became surrealists because they could not render the standard proportions of reality.

What makes her a poet-artist is that with and beyond geometric accuracy and beyond the power of minute craftsmanship in dealing with the microcosm, she has the non-euclidian sense of the unexpected pulsing of the macrocosm, of the spaces between the last tick-tock and the next, of those footprints which, as she says, are "face to face with the firmament." She may come to be known as an artist who created a whole population inhabiting the demonic underworld of the subconscious. But when you think of the demons, don't forget the angels she has also begotten. Those perfectly chiseled children's heads that peer at us from corners of the canvases, mingling their grace and wonder, their song of innocence with the explosive operations that dominate her universe.

Leonora Carrington is a poet because she is part of that final effort in our century to combat the forces that have been dislodging the millennial pact between nature and man. With the passing of anthropocentrism, so passes the language of analogies without which poets cannot thrive. Leonora Carrington preserves the metaphoric communication between humans and animals, and the cabbage and the rose, and the panther and the steed, all connected with a universal

animism. And she identifies the shepherd image not as the male poet which it has been since time immemorial, but as a woman leading the wandering herds over bridges back to the essential beginnings. See for instance *Pallatine Pradella* (1946).

If Leonora Carrington's work makes Breton's voice thunder in my ears: *"Il faut level l'interdit,"* I also hear the voice of William Blake in "Tiger, tiger burning bright:" that last line—"Did he who made the lamb make thee?" Over and beyond surrealism, Leonora Carrington is part of that line of poets of the occult and the labyrinthine—from Shakespeare and Blake to Novalis, Goethe, Beethoven, Mallarmé, Yeats, Breton—which forms a subterranean tradition against the *overt* traditions of the arts in Western civilization.

Leonora Carrington is part of that world of heretics. She is an extremely bold artist and dares to tread forbidden zones—which was the major precept of surrealism. ◯

A 44-page catalogue of Leonora Carrington's exhibition at the Center's Gallery, with 20 illustrations (9 in color), is available for $4.50 from: Gallery, Center for Inter-American Relations, 680 Park Avenue, New York, N.Y. 10021.

Puig's Last Picture Show

The Buenos Aires Affair
By Manuel Puig
Translated by Suzanne Jill Levine
E. P. Dutton, New York, 1976. $8.95

ALAN CHEUSE

Quotations from the scripts of fabulous Hollywood tear-jerkers, from Garbo's "Camille" to Susan Hayward's "I'll Cry Tomorrow," serve as diverting epigrams to each of the chapters of Manuel Puig's new novel (called both in its original Spanish edition of 1973 and in Jill Levines English version *The Buenos Aires Affair*). In Puig's earlier novels, *Betrayed by Rita Hayworth* and *Heartbreak Tango*, such passages dramatized states of happiness unattainable in provincial Argentina of the 1940s, the perennial illusions which led pathetic characters ever onward into a life of dreams and reinforced their subservience to a deformed and undesirable (though always cheerfully masked) way of life. In the debilitating atmosphere of Buenos Aires of the late 60s, such excerpts stand more as emblems of a world well lost than as signposts of the future. Movies and day-time serials no longer hold the popular mind in thrall, and Puig, always sensitive to the vagaries of popular taste, gives them over for the detective novel, a more appropriate vehicle for an inquest into the decline of a culture.

Since the form he parodies here is a literary one, rather than the visual and aural varieties of the first two books, it is easy for Puig to remain dutifully within the boundaries of the subgenre. The novel opens with a disappearance. We witness Clara Evelia D'Onofrio, a widowed poetess who creates "oral recitations" for dramatic readings, waking up in her vacation home in the South Atlantic resort of White Beach to find that her daughter Gladys, a sculptress, has disappeared. Gladys had returned home

ALAN CHEUSE teaches comparative literature at Bennington College.

to live with Mama after suffering a nervous breakdown during an extended stay in the U.S. She creates sculptures from driftwood and garbage she finds on the beach, and her success puts her in contact with art critic Leo Druscovich, the man who may be the putative criminal we see in the second chapter through the screen of a parody of Robbe-Grillet-like descriptive narrative. By the time we reach the third chapter, in which Puig offers us a capsule history of Gladys' life, we realize that the "crime" of this fiction is more diffuse than any single act.

NERVOUS PROBLEMS

From then on, until her return to Argentina four years later, Gladys had sexual intercourse with six men in the following order: I) Francisco or Frank, janitor at the company. . . .

Back in Washington, Gladys had difficulties in returning to her customary rhythm of life. She was especially bothered by the insomnia she brought back with her from Buenos Aires. . . .

The clinical tone of this carefully arranged history of a repressed, vaguely talented, middle-class Argentine woman with an affinity for North American culture is in itself a fact more valuable than any of the various information it conveys. However much it may remind us at first of the "hard-boiled" school of detective fiction, its implications extend far beyond the boundaries of this form. When for example Puig applies this technique to the life of Leo Druscovich, an actual murder becomes only one of a number of "events" in a clearly delineated personal pathology. Rather than focusing on the life of crime, Puig's narrative thus reveals that life among the Argentine bourgeois *is* the crime.

A multitude of narrative devices enhance this proposal: marginal commentary in the style of Coleridge's "Ancient Mariner" accompanies a dry account of Gladys' masturbatory fantasies; the second voice in a transcript of a two-party conversation about covering up a possible crime is omitted, replaced by blank space; police department reports, newspaper stories, and laboratory analyses, the most alienating modes possible, advance the progress of the "story"; hypothetical events become concrete narrative incidents; and oblique points of view (in the manner of Onetti and Donoso) emerge as textual realities. Out of such materials, the detritus of middle-class technology, Puig constructs a text not unlike Gladys' "garbage" sculptures in which the contradictory materials of Argentine society slowly reveal their intimate connections to the mystery of the *lack* of mystery in modern Argentine life:

The young wife could not suppress vocal expressions corresponding to her pleasure. The husband, stimulated, did his best to keep up his performance. During brief seconds he doubled his attacks but suddenly upon reducing the speed of his movements to a minimum, he made a felicitous erotic discovery. The young wife remembered movie scenes projected in slow motion and adapted the activity of her hands which moved over her husband's back to the same pace. . . .

Compared to such flat, pathetic renditions of life's most pleasant experiences, the movie scenes, "projected in slow motion" for us at the opening of each chapter, seem preposterous, if not themselves debased. Prior to this moment in the text, for example, we see a fragment of a scene from Columbia Pictures' "Gilda," starring Rita Hayworth, "dazzling in her gauze negligee with a revealing neckline, but profoundly disturbed since she has just found that her husband's new bodyguard is none other than the only man she ever loved in her life and by whom she was abandoned. . . ." The ironies of such juxtapositions reverberate throughout the text. But they remain subsidiary to the parody enhanced by Puig's use of detective fiction:

Medical Autopsy
Place: Baradero
Date: May 22, 1969
Name: Unknown
Description: Male, accident on route 9, driving car, overturned. . . .
Medical statement: corpse of a young man, in rigor mortis, skin white, hair brown, abundant on scalp, scanty fatty membrane.
By palpitation and percussion the gross in-

spection of the corpse reveals: traumatic wounds on the face, deep lacerations. . . .

Puig might be speaking here as a medical expert called in to rule on the cause of death of the Argentine body politic itself. Rigor mortis is endemic in the passionless, brutal, deluded Buenos Aires of 1969. The only positive notes come, ironically enough, in the form of terse newspaper accounts of urban guerrilla activity.

FREE LUNCH—A Guerrilla Commando Distributes Free Meat. . . .

URBAN GUERRILLAS ASSAULT BANK IN VILLA BOSCH

REPORT ON URBAN GUERRILLAS—Cordoba —In this city the report sent to headquarters by personnel of the 10th Precinct on the activities of the secret organization RAF (Revolutionary Army Forces) has been made public. . . .

Between the projector and the movie screen stalks the shadow of the urban guerrilla, the only possible liberating, if potentially destructive, force in the drab social round. Just as the larger-than-life creatures of the Hollywood pantheon blessed the creation of the naïve era of Puig's previous novels, these glimpses of the mysterious guerrillas point to the late, bourgeois world's impending demise. Puig hints at this early in the novel when he shows us Gladys' mother wandering through the streets of White Beach on the way to report her daughter's disappearance to the authorities:

Across the street was a small movie house, shut down by municipal order. She hadn't passed by there for a while. The closing sign was stuck on the posters and covered the title of the last movie shown. Without a valid reason Clara walked over and read the police notice, perhaps hoping that it contained some sign of her daughter's whereabouts. . . . The notice said only that the hall was being closed for reasons of public hygiene and safety.
There were also other governmental proclamations stuck to the façade which pressed for law and order and recommended the capture of activists listed there. . . .

The notice Puig himself puts up concerning Argentina's whereabouts does not fully obscure the titles of the last movie shown. But it places the campy stylistics of his earlier successes in a striking new perspective. *The Buenos Aires Affair* proclaims quite publicly that its author remains one of the most serious and daring young modernist American writers working today, north or south.

Unanimous Light

Poems by Isabel Fraire
Translation and Introduction by
Thomas Hoeksema
Mundus Artium Press, Athens, Ohio, 1975. $7

RAMON XIRAU
Translated by Gloria Waldman

It is not easy to situate the poetry of Isabel Fraire within the present-day panorama of Mexican Poetry. It is not easy for two reasons: 1) Isabel Fraire has always written—in a manner of speaking—with a silent voice; and, as Hoeksema notes in his introduction, she has only published her books – a third will soon appear—at the insistence of her friends, principally Tomás Segovia and Juan García Ponce; 2) Isabel Fraire's poetry is in many ways unique: it does not correspond to any school or generation.

Do we have to discover in her poems the influence of José Gorostiza—the original title of *Sólo esta luz* (Only This Light) comes from Gorostiza—or of Octavio Paz, as the translator notes in the introduction? Possibly. Perhaps. Even probably. But in her case the influences are so deeply integrated into a personal *obra* that it is difficult to isolate them. And is there an influence from the North American poets whom Isabel Fraire has translated so well into Spanish? That is equally possible and even probable —especially if you think of the Imagists. But the search for influences is, by and

RAMON XIRAU, the editor of *Diálogos*, was visiting professor at Columbia University and the City University of New York during the fall, 1975.

large, a merely academic quest, which, rather than bringing us closer to this poetry, distances us from it. One has to see the poems of Isabel Fraire and especially those of this second book in their own light: "only this light."

I have said that the poetic world of Isabel Fraire is unique. Her poems, sensitive with a vigilant and intelligent sensitivity, are poems for the eyes, for looking at and admiring. In them you discover the poet astonished by the world, by the kaleidoscope of images, the signs, the pure and transparent lines of a world constructed with a kind of pure and hidden light—the light of a suspicion: the suspicion of the Human Being.

Each of her poems is an indissoluble whole, an *imago mundi,* but this image—the image of light and above all of the source of light—is not always the image of a perfect world. In fact, the world of Isabel Fraire is filled with "labyrinths," "solitudes," movements (poetry in movement and movement of the poetic image within each poem), of a time that passes minute by minute, of "devouring nights," of a "wounded dove," of death more hinted at than explicitly named. In addition, there is passing, fleetingness, metamorphosis and traces that are erased in the very moment that they seem to become fixed. But there is also permanence. Following every road in this plural universe, Isabel Fraire arrives at unanimity—the single soul of the world: the light is every light, the poem is every poem:

El agua transparente
brota por fin
            idéntica a sí misma.
(Transparent water
fully gushes
            identical to itself.)

Apparently simple, Isabel Fraire's poetry is complex and rich in changes and variations, semantic as well as sonorous. Hers is poetry that weaves words and silences, verses and pauses, fullness and empty spaces, images that cross and interwine only to re-emerge crossed, references to other poets (also to other worlds and to other "stories") that do not become readily apparent on a first reading.

We all know that criticism does not take the place of actual reading. The critic only hopes to make the reader actually read the revised work and such is my hope here. Let the reader himself find in these poems works as wounding as live fire, clarities like those of the unclouded sun, words and pauses—word and song—like the waters, which along with the light, make up the imaginative universe of this poetry.

The English version by Thomas Hoeksema should be read. In this case, the translator knew how to see and understand the poet thoroughly, and succeeded in converting the poetry of Isabel Fraire into poetry in English without sacrificing the sense or the meaning of the original. The reader should also examine his introduction to this book, which previously appeared in *Review 73*, Fall, as "Isabel Fraire: The Startled Eye." This introduction is a model of careful and exact analysis and undoubtedly constitutes the best and most complete criticism yet written about the poetry of Isabel Fraire.

A final comment: all translated poetry should appear in a bilingual version because the best way to appreciate a translation fully is to compare it with the original. In the case of these poems that is also the best way for those who know only a little Spanish to be able to read Isabel Fraire with the ease as well as the accuracy that Hoeksema's translation offers—the accuracy that this distinctive, constant and unanimous "light" deserves.

A Ballad to Sing in the Streets

Tereza Batista, Home from the Wars
By Jorge Amado
Translated by Barbara Shelby
Alfred A. Knopf, New York, 1975. $10.00

CANDACE SLATER

Tereza Batista, Home from the Wars, Jorge Amado's nineteenth novel, is both like and unlike its predecessors. Well translated by Barbara Shelby, the book recalls the contemporary Brazilian author's other works in its slapdash use of local color and singing, colloquial language. Like its forebears, it is sometimes facile or longwinded. And yet, *Tereza Batista* is different. One of the things which distinguishes the novel from others by Amado is its particular use of Brazilian folk material.

Tereza Batista brings together two separate strands of "popular" culture. One, the African thread, runs throughout Amado's fiction, surfacing as a preoccupation with the sensuality as well as the rites and customs associated with the cult religion known in Bahia as *candomblé*. The other, the ballad strain, has been used less directly by the author on previous occasions. Rooted in the folk culture of the Northeastern backlands, this essentially oral tradition also takes the form of broadside-like pamphlets called *folhetos* or *literatura de cordel*. These booklets represent fully Brazilian descendants of the Iberian *romances* brought to the New World almost five hundred years ago. Although ballad singers or *cantadores* crop up in northeastern coastal cities, as well as in São Paulo and Rio de Janeiro, their verse continues to reflect the moraes and particular life style of the vast, dry interior, and over the past hundred years many Brazilian novelists have turned to this folk material for inspiration. By making use of the *folhetos*, Amado joins a host of other writers including José Lins do Rego, Rachel de Queiroz, Ariano Suassuna and Antônio Callado.

Tereza's life is a protracted struggle against "plague, famine, love and death." To write her off as the hackneyed prostitute with a heart of gold, however, is to miss Amado's point. In her martial stance against injustice, Tereza recalls the medieval *"Donzela que vai a Guerra,"* or "Maiden off to the Wars," reappearing as João Guimarães Rosa's Diadorim or Domingos Olímpio's Luzia Homem. In her near-fatal beauty, Tereza suggests the archetype behind Afrânio Peixoto's Maria Bonita. The life of

CANDACE SLATER teaches at The University of California, Santa Cruz.

Tereza Batista is, therefore, "a ballad to sing in the streets," as much of the novel's interest lies in the rather complex nature of its heroine's "popularity."

But Amado does not take over his *folheto* material without adjusting it to his own vision. Like her sisters in literature, Amado's protagonist is an individual. While modeled on the heroines of various *folhetos,* she does not obey the dictates of their puritanical, authoritarian society. Whereas the typical *"Louca do Jardim"* ("Crazy Woman of the Garden") wanders about for seven years until a slanderous charge of adultery can be disproven, Tereza works at will in brothels and cabarets. With a man she loves, sex is pleasure. Furthermore, her story involves not one, but a half-dozen men: Captain Justo, the sadistic strongman; Emiliano Guedes, the "good" *patrão;* Daniel, the false saviour; Oto Espinheira, the spineless medic; Almério das Neves, the good-hearted baker; and Januário Gereba, the sailor with whom Tereza goes on to live happily ever after. As a woman of easy morals, Tereza could not function as the heroine of a *folheto.* Courage and candor are not enough to dispel the stigma of illicit sex in the backlands. Although some *folhetos* do deal exclusively with picaresque or pornographic subjects (e.g. "The Story of an Oldster Who Struggled 72 Hours with a Gourd without Getting to the Bottom or Splitting the Sides"), frank sensuality, let alone intercourse for reasons other than procreation, has no place in didactic adventure narratives.

Clearly, the prohibition against sex for gain or pure pleasure mirrors societal taboos justified by a particular world view. In the universe of the ballads, good inevitably triumphs over evil. Because virtue is always ultimately rewarded, there is no justification for any form of misconduct: both good and bad men meet their just dessert. The individual who sells himself in order to eat fails the trial of temporary hardship, revealing an inexcusable lack of faith.

This world in which all ends well is not the world of Amado's novels. For the author, injustice is a continuing reality. While Tereza herself finally finds some promise of happiness, it is with a lowly mariner, not with some blue-blooded landowner who sallies forth to redress her numerous wrongs. The aunt who sells Tereza to the debauched captain, the deceitful lover and the cowardly doctor are never punished. The brave lawyer Lulu Santos loses the majority of his cases. The whores who risk their lives to save their fellow townsmen from a dread epidemic are thrust back into brothels as soon as the danger passes. Emiliano Guedes' efforts on the part of his family are rewarded with scorn. When Tereza finally stabs Captain Justo, his necklace of rings representing violated minors has become almost too heavy to wear. If Tereza sells her body, suggests Amado, it is because she can do nothing else. In recompense, she regains her virginity each time she falls in love.

In line with his non-*folheto*-like worldview, Amado sees good and evil as purely human qualities, questioning whether "the bravery of the *orixás,* the beauty of the shining angels and archangels, the goodness of God and the wickedness of Satan may not be only reflections of the bravery, the beauty, the goodness and the wickedness of men and women." As if to answer his own question, he invariably places evils which are foreign to the *folhetos* well within the hearts and minds of his characters. An excellent example of this relocation occurs in the case of Doña Brígida, mother of the tubercular Doris whose marriage to the lascivious Justo ends with her death in childbirth. Half crazed by guilt and sorrow, the old woman retires into a world inhabited by the Hog, Headless Mule, Jackal and Terto Cachorro. Stock figures whose physical reality is never questioned in the *folhetos,* the monsters function here as embodiments of an interior conflict. Within the forest of her own mind, Doña Brígida encounters her son-in-law in the guise of "Captain Hog, Devil, Father of Lies." Here, she repeatedly hands him her only daughter so that he may "suck her blood, crunch her bones, feast on her meager flesh."

Tereza's voluptuous nature, which Amado presents as the more "African" aspect of her character, leavens the relentless harshness of his vision. The author's emphasis on earthly pleasures—which include creative effort and friendship—as well as on the joys of the senses, affords consolation for the injustices and human weaknesses marring the existence he depicts. But it is Amado's vision of suffering, not his consolation through pleasure, that is seized on by the *cantador* Rodolfo Coelho Cavalcante in a *folheto* based on the novel. Here, the traditional poet reiterates Tereza's misfortunes, identifying his own lot with hers;

Se é que existe um inferno
este inferno está na Terra.
Quem sofreu como Tereza
Na verdade um mártir encerra
Tem razão o romancista
Chamar: Tereza Batista
Mulher Cançada de Guerra.

Me desculpe Jorge Amado
Se eu fui fraco trovador,
Mas o drama de Tereza
E o drama da minha dor.
Hoje Cançado de Guerra
Sofro aqui na sua terra

(If there is a hell,
this hell is here on earth.
Who suffered like Tereza
is indeed a martyr.
The author is right to call Tereza
"Woman Tired of War."

May Jorge Amado forgive me
if I have been an uninspired poet,
but the drama of Tereza
is the drama of my own sorrow.
Today, Tired of War,
I suffer here in her homeland,
the city of Salvador.)

That the trials of Tereza should inspire a writer of authentic *folhetos* is a tribute to Amado. *Tereza Batista* is not a major novel. Nevertheless, Tereza—and Amado—reveal a genuine capacity for suffering which explains and assures their humanity. ◯

The Poem that Exploded

The Antipoetry of Nicanor Parra
By Edith Grossman
New York University Press, 1975. $12.00

JOSE MIGUEL OVIEDO
Translated by Gregory Kolovakos

To document and analyze "Parra's distinctive use of colloquial language, the characteristic irony and burlesque that color his writing, the specific emotive efforts which he creates out of the flat prosaic tones of his linguistic raw material and the artistic commitments which nourish these techniques" is the stated purpose of Edith Grossman's recent study dedicated to the work of the Chilean poet Nicanor Parra. Her book is unquestionably opportune: it is the first of its kind in English despite the intense and far-reaching diffusion of his work throughout this country ever since a selection from his *Poems and Antipoems* appeared in 1960 in the City Lights Pocket Poet Series. Furthermore, there is only one antecedent in Spanish: Leonidas Morales' *La poesía de Nicanor Parra* published in Santiago, Chile, in 1972, since the studies by Hugo Montes and Mario Rodríguez (*Nicanor Parra y la poesía de lo cotidiano*, Santiago de Chile, 1970), although collected in one book, are not actually a book. Finally it is important to recognize that Edith Grossman has kept that promise made in her Preface: this is an in-depth study, concentrating on the aspects indicated, and quite polished in the reading of the texts themselves. All of which does not prevent some threads from hanging loose or certain components of the "antipoetic" phenomenon from remaining outside the range of her vision.

The principal body of Ms. Grossman's work is divided into three parts which study (1) the trajectory of antipoetry (there is a

JOSE MIGUEL OVIEDO, the Peruvian critic and essayist, is co-editor of the magazine *Después*. At present he is a visiting professor at Indiana University.

delicious error in the table of contents: instead of "Antipoetry" we find "Antipoverty"), (2) its theory and (3) its technique. Although this order creates several small problems for the reader (in each chapter one encounters superpositions, repetitions or announcements of what will be treated in other chapters), it adequately serves the author for organizing her material and presenting her central ideas concerning Parra's work.

Her concept of antipoetry is presented at the beginning of the Preface in a few sagacious words: "Antipoetry is a kind of verbalized found-art that uses ordinary objects and commonplace language, colors them with a sometimes mordant, often comic irony and views them in a decidedly unexpected way." Like the author, I believe that Parra's work basically conceives of poetry as a ready-made object, as an art based more on appropriation, displacement and reformulation of verbal elements from everyday language than on the invention of formal, "poetic" writing. It is difficult for the Anglo-American reader to imagine the insolence of Parra's gesture, because the Anglo-American reader's spoken and literary languages have never been as deeply separated as the two are in the Hispanic and Hispanic American tradition: centuries and centuries of rhetoric have created an abyss of noncommunication between the two. Various efforts to bridge this distance have occurred in Spanish poetry (perhaps the greatest is that of Vallejo, beginning with *Trilce* in 1922) but Parra's effort is doubtlessly the most programmatic and radical in this particular direction.

Within the context of traditional lyric poetry, the effect of antipoetry is as disconcerting as a slap in the face of Poetry and as devastating as an explosion in a crystal shop. Simultaneously, Parra's basic attitude has been that of a terrorist and a lunatic: the weapon he points at us is terrifying, but absurdly loaded with blanks, and this joke throws an acidic, naked light on our true situation which does not cease to be ridiculous even if it is distressing. This unmentionable mixture of humor and horror with which the human condition and the contemporary world are viewed is the most

characteristic contribution of antipoetry and the unchallengeable symptom of its modernity: in antipoetry—in its deliberate indifference to greatness, in its prosaic quality, in its dissonant tones and in its grotesque descriptions—we immediately recognize the tragedy of our time—the tragedy of being Nobody in a world hostile to any individual. The burlesque elements, the shameless commonplaces, the effects of surprise and the departures from established tone are exasperated forms of resistance to the subjugating forces of civilization as well as affirmations of the possibility of a more human existence.

First examining the poetic evolution of Parra, Ms. Grossman shows how, through the initial influence of García Lorca, the author proposes three principal objectives: "to free poetry from the domination of the metaphor," to "reject the rarified and exotic, both thematically and linguistically" and "to localize the language of antipoetry so that it would reflect a specific social reality." Decisive for the definition of his creative personality, she correctly points to his reading of Kafka (Parra will later say "Kafka is a creator of atmospheres. That's important in my poetry too. My formulations are irrelevant in themselves") but she rather quickly passes over the ambiguous relationship between antipoetry and surrealism which should have been clarified; Parra himself affirmed that the antipoem is no more than "the traditional poem enriched by the surrealist vitality," but antipoetry is, in a certain sense, a critique of surrealist poetry—in the Latin American mode.

With regard to the trajectory of ten years between *Versos de salón* (1962) and *Artefactos* (1972) and also considering the debatable *Canciones rusas* of 1968, Ms. Grossman refers in the final pages of this chapter to Parra's "explicit political involvements of the 1960s." It would have been ideal if she had explained, in order to better inform the American public, that fundamentally those "political involvements" are his conflicting relations with the Cuban Revolution and the Allende government, of which there are numerous indications (including some of the *artefactos*) that Ms. Grossman surely knows about. To judge from the information included in the poet's biographical note, Ms. Grossman's work seems to have been finished about 1973, so it would have been suitable to add several lines in order to describe Parra's rejection of a poet's stance in relation to the military dictatorship in Chile, which has lent itself to so many misconceptions.

The other two parts of the work are essentially textual analyses, generally very thorough and correct, possibly the best and the most complete that have been made of Parra's antipoems. In "The Theory of Antipoetry," Ms. Grossman interprets three texts ("Warning to the reader," "Changes of Name" and "Manifesto") that are "for the most part comic statements of Parra's poetic theory, and excellent examples of the practice of antipoetry." These anlyses permit her to study extensively the relationship between the comicalness of Parra and of Aristophanes; his rejection of the linguistic and philosophical tradition of his time, a gesture which joins him to Wittgenstein; the putting into practice his principle that "Real seriousness is comic" by means of a series of modes of implacable humor (mockery, self-imitation, incongruence, irrelevance, parody, etc.). She gives special attention to "Manifesto," a singular work in Parra's antipoetic repertory because—as she observes—it has to do with an "emphatically propagandistic" text lacking the humor typical of the rest of his work and leading him, above all else, to a theoretical dead end: "He defends poetry as a communal art in which the poet records the social artifact of language, and he defends with equal vigor the concept of the artist as the originator and adventurous creator of a new poetic language."

Ms. Grossman's presentation of this point once again brings up one of the most disputed aspects of Parra: that of the double ideological and esthetic perspective (antibourgeois poetry, "proletarian" poetry) from which his texts strive to function as documents of social criticism. The similarities and dissimilarities of Parra and Neruda (principally the Neruda of the *Odas elementales*) which the author examines, are very pertinent in this respect. But, on the other hand, there is no mention of the anarchistic thought which especially has a substantial influence on Parra's most recent period and about which until now nothing has been said. The anarchistic spirit of antipoetry perhaps allows us to understand some of its most disconcerting extremes and to judge whether Parra's work has obtained the objectives which it proposes. For example, Ms. Grossman points out "the overwhelming individualism of his grammar," which seems to me to be exact, but later she affirms that "depersonalized poetry is clearly one of Parra's artistic goals." I think that the immersion in everyday language does not presume, for him, his depersonalization but, on the contrary, the discovery of an authentic instrument of *personal* communication. Against the language of the masses, Parra opposes the utopia of an intersubjective language. In relation to his critique of language, it would have been interesting if she had paid attention to the similarities between antipoetry and *anti-theâtre:* apart from the participation of a certain "spirit of the times" (the first antipoems were written in the mid-40s, the theater of the absurd is a phenomenon which becomes visible in the 50s), the exercise of black humor and the systematic rupture of logic and rationality justify a comparative study.

As a point of departure for studying "The Techniques of Antipoetry," Ms. Grossman establishes the premise that "language that is not emotively congruous with the subject matter is a basic component of the structure of antipoetry." The tone, she adds, differs from the content of the antipoem: an anguished feeling is expressed in banal phrasing, pain inspires laughter, the protagonist exhibits his weakness as an object of mockery. Parra's art consists of working basically on the connotative levels of language and of emphasizing "the differences between the prosaic, comic signs and the tragic, pathetic signs so that the reader is constantly aware of their ironic incompatibility." The double effect—first, a type of distancing, then a process of identification and recognition—which antipoetry creates in the reader, is described with great accuracy by Ms. Grossman. Despite their trivial appearance, all these aspects imply a very complex structure which she purposefully dismantles in the analysis of seven texts from *Poems and Antipoems.* Her selection is proper because these poems actually "form a thematic unit" and have a paradigmatic structure. But, precisely because this analysis is both extensive and detailed, the reader of the book may lament the fact that Ms. Grossman has not attempted to extend her study to other books or to later works by Parra so as to observe diachronically the well-known structural simplification which leads to the *artefactos.*

Indicated as the principal emblems in this group are the defective perception of the concrete human situation, the lack of contact with reality, the image of imprisonment, the association of sexuality with feelings of death, desolation and viscosity in order to create a sinister and humiliating atmosphere. Also pointed to in the series is an internal movement leading from an initial obscurity and isolation to the vision of an exit and a possible liberation—only attainable with difficulty. Several small questions of detail in these interpretations may be raised. For example, the verbal forms of *volved, olvidad* and other similar ones which Parra uses in "The Pilgrim" are not, as Ms. Grossman, believes, "intimate forms of address"; on the contrary: especially in Latin America, they are solemn and affected. Nor is *ustedes* "the formal third person," but rather the second and more common form of the plural. With regard to the same poem, she maintains that the lines "*Un alma que ha estado embotellada durante años/ En una especie de abismo sexual e intelectual/ Alimentándose escasamente por la nariz*" ("A soul that has been bottled up for years/ In a sort of sexual and intellectual abyss,/ Nourishing itself most inadequately through the nose") suggests "a lack of tangible experience which Parra associates with metaphysical and abstract speculations: The only thing that can be 'eaten' through the nose is smoke or the aroma of food," and she links that verse with one that says "*Soy un peregrino que hace saltar las piedras a la altura de su nariz*" ("I'm

a pilgrim who makes stones jump as high as his nose") because it indicates that "the protagonist feeds on his own sorrow." The relation between *comer-nariz* and *piedras-nariz* is misleading: the second one has nothing to do with eating (not even figuratively) but rather with an image of self-aggression that is corroborated by the earlier absurd situation: like a patient, he is fed through the nose. Otherwise, the comic effect of his mentioning that corporeal organ is rather obvious.

Despite the errors or omissions that can be found in it, the best of this book amply accomplishes its goal of introducing the antipoetic world of Parra to the North American reader. Ms. Grossman's effort is as considerable as it is useful for the better understanding of the work of this Chilean poet. As Alexander Coleman suspects in his provocative introduction, Ms. Grossman's work "will lead to a re-evaluation of Parra's esthetic deviancy." I am sure of that and would therefore like to see this work quickly translated into Spanish.

More Prose on Tamayo

Rufino Tamayo
By Emily Genauer
Harry N. Abrams, Inc., New York, 1974.
$37.50

JACQUELINE BARNITZ

No one else has been the subject of as much baroque rhetoric as Tamayo, who himself identified his art with baroque, "non-intellectual" painting and once said that he preferred Luis Cardoza y Aragon's account of his work to Robert Goldwater's. (Goldwater, to whom Tamayo has jokingly referred as "Cold Water," wrote an objective, scholarly study, while Cardoza y Aragon transferred his own poetic approach to Tamayo's art.) Now Emily Genauer, winner of the 1973 Pulitzer Prize for art criticism, comes along with yet another baroque version, supplemented by copious quotations taped during her visits to the artist's studios in Cuernavaca and Mexico City.

But this handsome coffee-table book offers a mixed bag of blessings. It is not, as the blurb on the jacket announces, the first comprehensive study of Tamayo in English but it is certainly the most recent. As the bibliography at the back of the book indicates, Tamayo has been the source of many musings in English, French and Spanish, among which are monographs by Justino Fernández, Enrique Gual, Raymond Cognat and Octavio Paz, all published in, or prior to, 1959. Both Octavio Paz's and Cardoza y Aragon's versions have English, French and Spanish texts. In most cases the illustrations in these earlier books are of poor quality, so while Genauer's text has multiple flaws, her book is unique in the excellent quality of its color illustrations—54 altogether. The 78 black and white plates, on the other hand, are not exceptional but then Tamayo's paintings are unusually difficult to photograph successfully in black and white because they depend so much on his exquisite color orchestration and close tonal values. To print all the plates in full color would have been too costly, and the choice of which works to reproduce in color and which in black and white seems a wise one. *Animals* for example—already well-known and easily accessible in the Museum of Modern Art—is reproduced in black and white while many of the more recent and lesser known works are in color. Moreover, enough of the early works are in color to offer a coherent visual survey of the evolution of Tamayo's painting from the muted clay tones in *Factory* (1929), *Woman in Grey* (1931), *Sunday in Chapultepec* (1934), *Women of Oaxaca* (1938), to the higher-keyed and more analogous colors of the last thirty years' work as in *Meeting* (1960), *The Offering* (1969), and *Three Personages No. 2* (1970). Except for the paintings directly referred to in the text, the illustrations are in a separate section at the back, followed by a biographical outline and a selected bibliography as already mentioned.

These features alone are sufficient to make this a valuable, updated source of in-

formation. But outside of an occasional insightful comment—most often contributed by Tamayo himself—the rambling, sometimes confused text adds little to what has already been said about the artist. While the book works well enough when Genauer relates straight biographical facts—her coverage of Tamayo's life in New York in the thirties, the people he met, his hardships, successes and the key paintings and mural commissions that helped to make his reputation are all quite clear—she gets into trouble when generalizing about Tamayo's work in broad mythic and cosmic metaphors. For example, "Tamayo," she says, "is painting human figures seemingly skinned alive by a world they made themselves. Now totally vulnerable, stripped of substance and flesh (as literally human beings were in some ritual sacrifices of ancient Mexico), they stand trembling and shaking like machines in a space charged with hostility. They wander moonstruck (surely Tamayo feels the moon as powerfully as the French Impressionists felt the sun) in a place of perpetual night and nameless terror, under skies alive with menacing labyrinths of nebulae about to explode. Sometimes they reach desperately to the stars. Sometimes they bellow in diabolic exultation." Genauer alludes to important pre-Hispanic cults here, but we have learned nothing of Tamayo's work that is not quite evident in the paintings themselves.

Then, too, there are minor bits of misinformation. Siqueiros, for example, is mentioned as one year older than Tamayo instead of three (an error even perpetrated in the records of the New York Public Library); and in Tamayo's quotation about Rivera's and Siqueiros' European travels in the second decade of this century, his statement that Orozco never traveled could be misleading. While Orozco did not go to Europe in the teens like the other two muralists, he did make the first of many trips to the United States in 1917. These minor issues—at least minor to non-scholars—should have been the responsibility of the editor if not of the author.

It is more difficult, though, to forgive those multiple redundancies which stretch the text unnecessarily. For instance, Genauer quotes Tamayo as saying, "The artist must . . . portray the moment in which he is living." Three pages further, the same statement reappears within a long quotation of Tamayo's. Then Genauer further informs us that "he has held to the conviction that his painting must grow out of the social realities of our time. . . ." Likewise, the circumstances of Tamayo's first job at the Museum of Anthropology in 1921 (which he obtained through his friend, José Vasconcelos, who was famous for promoting the muralist movement while acting as Minister of Education in 1911) are mentioned in three places—once in a quotation by Tamayo and twice in Genauer's text. Even though the context in each case is slightly different, these repetitions could have easily been avoided had the text been more carefully edited. One of the problems is that Genauer sometimes includes segments from Tamayo's statements which have more than one theme and thus are too extensive to incorporate coherently into her own text. Later, she elaborates further on these segments, perhaps not remembering that Tamayo has already said something similar.

Obviously an admirer of Octavio Paz, whom she also quotes, Genauer has apparently attempted to match Paz's interpretations of the Mexican mind through a study of Tamayo's personality and work. But her writing is often suspiciously flavored with Anglo-Saxon romanticism, which is hardly Paz's style and furthermore her vision has little or none of Paz's depth of perception. Tamayo's comments are for the most part those of a painter, not of a poet, and consequently fully excusable when less than original. He says, "I'm praying that a new kind of humanism may emerge, in which man, harnessing the technology he has invented, lives more fully as a man. I am haunted by fear that technology will reduce men and women to robots and calculating machines, if it even lets them live at all." But then Genauer adds that Tamayo sees machinery "in big mythic terms, as an implacable devastating force looming over men almost, one gathers, as he feels the gods loomed over ancient Mexico, where

they were the sources of light, energy, rain, fire—all the gifts men required to live—but also regularly demanded cruel blood sacrifices. Technology to him is the root of present-day man's great dilemma, the cause of his frailty and fear, but at the same time the instrument by which he can rise above himself and his present needs."

With less gush and more clarity, she discusses Tamayo in the context of contemporary European art where she situates him in a category with Picasso, Braque, Matisse and Klee in order to illustrate their parallel esthetic concerns. Whether one wants to question these comparisons or not matters little here. The important fact is that Tamayo's contribution of an original synthesis of color and form, as well as of American influences, represented to many young artists in Mexico an esthetic liberation from the restrictions they felt the muralist tradition had imposed on art in their country. Tamayo was also a model to artists outside of Mexico, especially in the Andean countries of South America where artists saw in his style an answer to their own search for a truly autonomous art that fused the contemporary world with their Ibero-American traditions.

In spite of the profusion of writings on his work, Tamayo still remains an obscure and enigmatic figure to many. As a personal friend of the Tamayos, Emily Genauer had a good opportunity to bring some fresh insights into her account of this apparently simple, deeply complex personality—the personification of Paz's Mexican character with a thin overlay of western sophistication. But despite Genauer's very personal approach and informal narrative style with its descriptions of Tamayo's varying facial expressions, we learn only a little more than we knew before. Tamayo retains his Mexican mystique, still shrouded in baroquisms.

JACQUELINE BARNITZ, art critic and lecturer, teaches Latin American art history at the State University of New York, Stony Brook.

Cortázar from this Side

Julio Cortázar
By Evelyn Picon Garfield
Modern Literature Monographs
Frederick Ungar Publishing Co., 1975. $7.00

Currents in the Contemporary Argentine Novel
By David William Foster
University of Missouri Press, 1975. $10.00

AMBROSE GORDON, JR.

Perhaps with more real conviction than most of us, and in violation of the Aristotelian verities, Julio Cortázar inhabits two places at once. At least the inhabitants of his fantastic—and yet quite realistic—stories do, having a characteristic way of being Here and There at one and the same witched time. Or perhaps, rather, it is space that is bewitched, as we are disturbingly faced with the kind of elastic world where (the words are Cortázar's) "a person who rang the doorbell of a house on the Calle Cochabamba [in Buenos Aires], at number twelve hundred, would be able to open the door into a courtyard of Menander's house in Pompeii." That is very much the world that Cortázar opens to us in his stories.

Those who know his work with affection will realize it is more than a trick, just as those spaces of his are more than a little like the space envisaged by Martin Heidegger, with (in his case) full Germanic and professorial sobriety: "When I go toward the door of the lecture hall," Heidegger writes, "I am already there. . . . I am never here only, as this encapsulated body; rather, I am there, that is, I already pervade the room and," he adds with a kind of lovely dream logic, "only thus can I go through it."

In the first book to appear in English on the contemporary Argentine-French novelist

and short story writer, Evelyn Garfield has designated Cortázar's spatial anomalies as "magnetic fields, or 'figures' as Cortázar calls them." They are, she tells us, "associative configurations" (of the near and the distant, or, more properly, of This Side and the Other Side), "reverberating chains of events" through which we are caused to see "holes in daily existence" or, alternatively, "unexpected dimensions in a recognizably mundane reality." In this connection Garfield analyzes several of Cortázar's stories, including the early *Lejana* where Alina Reyes, a good *porteña*, is first playfully and then fatally attracted to her double, a beggar woman in Budapest, and the shorter and later *Axolotl* where a man contemplates a fish in a tank with such fixed attention that he ends by finding himself on the other side of the glass. The stories, four gatherings of them, compose the necessary background, and Garfield devotes approximately half her book to "placing" them in relation to what she calls Cortázar's "Swiss cheese reality" (in other words, a reality with holes in it) and only then goes on to investigate his four novels, *Los premios, Rayuela, 62: Modelo para armar,* and *Libro de Manuel* (or in their English titles *The Winners, Hopscotch, 62: A Model Kit,* and *Book of Manuel*).

Quite properly in my opinion, Garfield makes the highest claims for *Rayuela (Hopscotch)*. To describe it, she concedes, "would require either one word—brilliant—or at least 636 pages—one more than in the original Spanish version of the novel." The book is famous, or notorious, for having two "endings," indeed two complete structures. It can be read either from the beginning straight through to the completion of Chapter 56 (where the hero seems to be going out of the window of an insane asylum, three floors up) or it may be read as a much longer book by interpolating various "expendable chapters" hopscotch fashion (73, 1, 2, 116, 3, etc.) according to a Table of Instructions given at the start. It is a tale of two cities, first Paris and then Buenos Aires, whose two discrete spaces appear to infiltrate one another, and not merely in the consciousness of the central character. This doubleness is further mirrored in the dis-

AMBROSE GORDON, JR., who teaches English at The University of Texas, Austin, is the author of *The Invisible Tent: The War Novels of Ford Madox Ford.*

crete, yet overlapping, narrative structures that make up *Rayuela*.

Garfield has a sure touch in examining these and other related matters in her lucid, informed, accurate, and on the whole remarkably helpful book. The only weakness that occurs to me as worth noticing is this: Garfield never quite says what Cortázar means by *figure*, while holding it out as a key term to unlock his work. She tells us it is a kind of "constellation"; yes, but in what galaxy? Religious? Psychological? Ontological? Fictive? Perhaps any one of these or all?

In talking to Luis Harss (see *Into the Mainstream*, pp. 227, 236) Cortázar has touched on these matters: "I think we all compose figures. For instance, we at this moment may be part of a structure that prolongs itself at a distance of perhaps two hundred meters from here, where there might be another corresponding group of people like us who are no more aware of us than we are of them. I'm constantly sensing the possibility of certain links, of circuits that close around us, interconnecting us in a way that defies all rational explanation and has nothing to do with the ordinary human bonds that join people. . . . I'd like to write in such a way that my writing would be full of life in the deepest sense, full of action and meaning, but a life, action, and meaning that would no longer rely exclusively on the interaction of individuals, but rather on a sort of superaction involving the 'figures' formed by a constellation of characters." Cortázar adds: "I realize it isn't at all easy to explain this. . . ." And apparently it isn't.

Possibly because David Foster does not consider *Rayuela* in the context of Cortázar's stories, such questions are simply never raised in his panoramic overview, *Currents in the Contemporary Argentine Novel*, which includes chapters on Roberto Arlt, Eduardo Mallea, and Ernesto Sábato. The longest chapter is devoted to *Rayuela* and, compared to Garfield, I find it a disappointing performance. The thrust of Cortázar's novel for Foster seems to be mainly satiric. He tells us in his confident and downright fashion: "*Hopscotch* is not only

in great part a spoof of the existential ethos that has become so trite in our nuclear society, but it is also the means to strike some heavy blows against the fawning New-World attachment to Paris, that putative intellectual center of the Western world." Perhaps, although this strikes me as a strange and improbable reading. (If Cortázar in fact does not like Paris, why in heaven's name has he chosen to live there?) Moreover, I receive the strong impression from Foster of a certain hastiness and carelessness about details on the part of a critic really not very sympathetic either to the author or to the work under consideration. In this regard, I have compiled a small list of what appear to be errors of fact. For example, Foster says, "Chapters 55, 57 and 59 are not mentioned in the Table of Instructions," while in fact 57 and 59 *are* mentioned and are placed between Chapters 30 and 70 and 40 and 41 respectively. Additional examples might be offered of what, at the very least, seem to be lapses of attention; but where this sort of thing may substantiate the charge of careless reading on the part of the critic, it also makes for very dull reading for the reader and, to pursue it, would require more space than presently at my disposal.*

As probably the most interesting international writer since Nabokov, and the hardest to tack down in one place or posture—playful and committed conjointly—Cortázar is still relatively unknown to North American readers. These two short studies, although of unequal merit, should help to point the way. ◯

---

*So, on p. 102 Foster writes: "When *Oliveira returns to Buenos Aires* [Italics mine] at the close of the first part of the novel, his mental ramblings on the game of hopscotch reveal a subconscious awareness of the futility of his favorite games." This is followed by an extended quotation from Chapter 36. But, as those familiar with the novel will remember, in fact we are still in Paris (as much as we ever were): Horacio is musing on hopscotch while he is riding in a French paddy wagon—along with Emmanuèle, who is mentioned in the passage—on their way to jail.

Reviews in Brief

BRUCE ALLEN

The Gilberto Freyre Reader. Translated by Barbara Shelby. Knopf. $7.95.

"Sampler" is probably a better word, for many of these terse selections—culled from the Brazilian polymath's writings on sociology, education, politics, literature, and related topics—are less than a page long. Also, it appears some of Shelby's "translations" are, more precisely, new renderings of older ones (by other translators). Perhaps she should be credited with *assembling* this book? The point is that the whole gives off the quality of patchwork; that it is saved from mere garble only by Freyre's heroic commitment to the role of social historian as a virtually *shamanistic* burden one picks up, as a duty he pays to his people.

Thus: Freyre values literature insofar as it participates in an unified cultural response to life's challenges. He celebrates the innovative city of Brasilia as an idealized symbolic expression of its country's "sensibility." In both anthropological essays (especially, in those masterpieces *Order and Progress* and *The Mansions and the Shanties*) and backward looks at his own childhood, Freyre reshapes his nation's modern history into a multilevelled vision which captures the universal experience, as microcosm, within the individual one. As rigid families restrict their children; as patriarchy represses the possible totality of a country's instinctual responses; so does "colonisation" necessitate—and proliferate—slavery. It is that specific. Much as Shelby's *Reader* rambles, her author's determined grasp of such unities proves him a significant and necessary writer, in large and small moments of expression alike.

BRUCE ALLEN is a free-lance reviewer who writes for *Library Journal* and *Hudson Review*.

Toward the Splendid City (Nobel Lecture). By Pablo Neruda. Bilingual edition (translation by the Nobel Committee). Noonday (pb). 1974. 1.95.

When Neruda received the Nobel Prize, he responded with this dreamlike, mythicized account of a personal journey, *northward*, accompanied by a band of countrymen, through his native Chile. The story is a metaphoric statement of Neruda's progress as an artist, through his deepening involvement in "the common life." He speaks of his poems as "tangible objects," even "working instruments"; *tools*, with which he makes himself a craftsman/activist, bluntly committed to a political vision (". . . my duties as a poet involve friendship not only with the rose and with symmetry, with exalted love and endless longing, but also with unrelenting human occupations . . ."). My only cavil with this moving little pamphlet is the suspicion that working readers throughout the world should unite to protest Noonday's outrageous asking price.

Contemporary Latin American Short Stories. Edited by Pat McNees Mancini. Fawcett Premier (pb). 1974. $1.75.

First of all, it's a stupendous bargain: thirty-five stories, featuring the most important writers (such as Borges, Carpentier, Cortázar, Fuentes, Onetti) and traditions which represent the territory it covers. Mancini provides brief headnotes summarizing each author's career, and appends a generous list of Further Readings—Reference and Criticism, Short Story Anthologies, A Basic Collection of Novels.

The first story is Machado de Assis's "Midnight Mass," a beautifully understated initiation story. Those that follow, chart the movement of the century's writers out and away from traditionalism. There are regional protest stories (by Amado, Icaza, Pedro Juan Soto); several pieces by modernist poets (Paz, Darío, Lugones); acknowledged masterpieces of realism/surrealism (Guimarães Rosa's "The Third Bank of the River," Vargas Llosa's chilling "Sunday"). The varieties of stories worked out through irony and fantasy are exciting and enticing —from Horacio Quiroga's animal fable, on toward the Nabokovan indirection and "doubleness" practiced by contemporary masters like Clarice Lispector and Manuel Puig. Not at all incidentally, Mancini's Introduction emphasizes the seminal importance of García Márquez's epical fantasy, *One Hundred Years of Solitude*, on the

Latin American fiction written during the past decade.

For a tantalizing surprise, and a fine example of the "best" which are here, begin by reading Juan Rulfo's "Talpa." You won't put the book away until you've read all the others as well. For the money, there is nothing else in English that compares with this remarkably comprehensive anthology. ◯

NEWS

Report from Two Congresses

ANGELA B. DELLEPIANE
Translated by Andrée Conrad

The Department of Hispanic American Literature of the Complutense University of Madrid was in charge of organizing the Seventeenth Congress of the International Institute of Ibero-American Literature, which took place in the Spanish capital and in Seville from the 20th to the 26th of March, 1975. This is the first time the Congress has been held in Madrid since its inception in Mexico City in 1938. The Spanish organizers' decision to have some of the sessions in Seville and Huelva (significant points on the Spanish map for the Americanist) contributed in great measure to the success of this Congress. The organization directing the Congress was the Institute of Hispanic Culture, whose cordial welcome and generosity were manifested in the valuable publications and commemorative medallions given to all visitors. For the sessions conducted in Andalucía, Seville University, the University of Santa María de la Rábida, and the National Delegation of Culture lent their aid. The President of the Organizing Committee was Dr. Francisco Sánchez-Castañer, professor of Hispanic-American Literature at the Complutense University; he was assisted by Dr. Luis Sáinz de Medrano, also professor in that department.

The inaugural lecture was delivered by Mr. Luis Rosales, Member of the Academy of Language. Since the theme of the Congress was "The Baroque and the Neo-Baroque in Hispanic American Literature," Mr. Rosales spoke on "Metaphor on Góngora." Afterwards, a wine-party hosted by the Complutense University of Madrid allowed the critics, professors, writers, graduate students, and special guests to get acquainted with one another.

That same afternoon, in classrooms at the Complutense, five different workshops were in session simultaneously. These were followed on Friday by more workshops. On Saturday, the sessions were held at the Institute of Hispanic Culture, whose Director, Mr. Juan Ignacio Tena, opened a book exhibit comprised of a selection from the Institute's Library of one hundred fifty priceless volumes that were printed in or refer to Hispanic America and deal especially with literature, philology and history. The workshops continued Monday and Tuesday at the Department of Philosophy and Letters at Seville University. At all sessions, papers dealing with the theme of the Congress were read and discussed. But other topics were presented too: The historical-literary narrative of the Indies, the latest works in Hispanic American poetry and drama, the latest critical trends. Some of the papers were original contributions, new critical approaches. During the workshops a total of one hundred twenty-five papers were read; the number of participants was more than two hundred, among them writers of international reputation and great popularity in Spain, such as Agustín Yáñez (President of the Mexican Academy of Language), the Uruguayan Juan Carlos Onetti, the Puerto Rican Enrique Laguerre, and the Spaniard

José Luis Castillo Puche, as well as the Peruvian Luis Alberto Sánchez.

The conclusion of the Congress took place in the Palacio Municipal of Huelva. After speeches by the Mayor of Huelva, Drs. Saínz de Medrano, Sánchez Castañer, and Professor Peter Earle (President of the Board of Directors of the Institute[1]), Agustín Yáñez closed the Congress with an address on "The Baroque in the Arts and Letters of Mexico," in which he underlined, among other aspects, the difference between the European and the Indian sensibilities, which since the sixteenth century have commingled their opposing manners of viewing and practicing the Baroque in Mexico; they are expressive of an idiosyncratic style being formed that is equidistant from both original creative drives and is particularly visible in the plastic arts and in poetry.

Later, during the luncheon given at La Rábida, Professor Alfredo A. Roggiano, Publications Director of the International Institute and President of the Nominations Committee, presented a historical sketch of the Institute, emphasizing its autonomous nature, independent of economic aid from any institution or government, and its totally international and cultural character, free from ideological compromise or partisan activity. Professor Roggiano has directed the Institute's official publication, *Revista Iberoamericana,* since 1955. The Institute has also published a collection called "American Classics" (interrupted for economic reasons), has held Congresses in Mexico, Cuba, Canada, Peru, Venezuela and the United States, and hopes to hold others in the future in various European and Asian countries. The papers read at the Congresses of the International Institute are published in separate volumes of *Memorias;* these represent a very extensive body of Hispanic American literary criticism. Professor Roggiano also alluded to the fact that this is the first year that Spain has hosted this Congress, thanks to his initiative, seconded by the members of the Board of Directors and the 1973 General Assembly of Members. "This has been not only a sumptuous and brilliant Congress; it is also the beginning of a new life leading towards a deeper and truer understanding of the Hispanic character as a means to self-realization, to comprehending life, to interpreting the world. This Institute," Professor Roggiano concluded, "is the most important organization laboring on behalf of the Hispanis world as a unity of thought and a plurality of experiences, within a human and cultural relationship that respects all values that contribute to the affirmation of the human condition."

Apart from the intellectual benefits resulting from the exchange of ideas among serious professionals, apart from the visits to Córdoba, its mosque and Alcázar; to Seville, its processions of "Cofradías" in Holy Week, its great cathedral, its famous Archive of the Indies; to the Convent of La Rábida; to Palos de Moguer and the house of Juan Ramón Jiménez—experiences deeply meaningful to all of us—there were other events that made this Congress a cultural event of particular importance, and these ought to be mentioned. First, the frank colloquy with the writers. Yáñez, Laguerre, Castillo Puche were in constant demand, but especially Onetti, usually so difficult to approach, was this time much more accessible, although he was more immersed than ever in his nightmares and obessions, after his unjust imprisonment in his native country. In Spain, Onetti has become a well-known writer, appreciated as he deserves to be, and in great demand for countless radio, television and newspaper interviews. Spain has received him with open arms, and he has welcomed this hospitality at a time when he needs peace of mind in order to continue writing. Another "fringe benefit" of the Congress: the reunion of Hispanic Americans and Spaniards dedicated to the study of our continent's literature, and the interchange of ideas leading toward a necessary critical renewal and to the unification of the Hispanic world.

The Institute's Congresses have always had two phases: one in a Spanish- or Portuguese-speaking capital or city, and the other at a North American university. The second phase of this year's Congress, held in Philadelphia from August 24 to 30, was hosted by the University of Pennsylvania.[2] The theme was "Surrealism in Ibero-American Literature."

After Professor Peter Earle's words of welcome, the opening session on Sunday the 24th, consisted of a round table discussion at which three papers on the theme of the conference were read. The moderator was Professor Ricardo Gullón (University of Texas at Austin), and the panelists were Professors Jaime Alazraki (University of California at San Diego), Emir Rodríguez Monegal (Yale University) and Anna Balakian (New York University). It was particularly interesting to hear a specialist in comparative literature of the caliber of Anna Balakian say that the future of Surrealism is in Hispanic America.

On Monday, Tuesday, Thursday and Friday morning, workshops were held at which a total of fifty papers were read on Surrealism in poetry, drama, and fiction, and Surrealism in Central America, Peru, Chile, Argentina and Mexico. Of particular interest were sessions devoted to Pablo Neruda, Jorge Luis Borges and the Surrealism in Brazilian and Spanish literatures.

Some of the outstanding personalities at the conference were the Chilean poet Enrique Gómez-Correa, a member of the Mandrágora group, one of the most coherent and important schools of Hispanoamerican Surrealism; the Argentine poet Enrique Molina, who with Aldo Pellegrini founded *A partir de cero* (Starting from Zero), the magazine that brought the Argentine Surrealists together. Molina, a reserved and modest man, revealed his spirit and fundamental nonconformity in a colloquium on the subject of "Poetry and Surrealism" with Gómez-Correa, the Brazilian poet Fernando Ferreria de Loanda, and Mexican writer José Emilio Pacheco, as moderator. This colloquium contributed to revealing the circumstances of Surrealism's arrival in Latin America and the particular characteristics of the so-called *Boom*. Donoso, generous and critic Cedomil Goić lectured on the same subject. Georgette Dorn of the Library of Congress described the library's collection of Latin American poetry and prose in an informative talk. Another highlight was a concert of contemporary music of both

Americas, made possible through the generosity of the Curtis Institute of Music and conducted by Peter H. Schoenbach.

The last evening's colloquium between Chilean novelist José Donoso and panelists C. Goić, Alicia Borinsky and José Emilio Pacheco allowed the large audience to approach one of the most worthwhile writers of the so-called *Boom*. Donoso, generous with his time, gave thoughtful and satisfying answers to the many questions addressed to him.

In sum: If this Congress on Surrealism in Ibero-American Literature was not able to answer all questions, it at least gathered together many people interested in the subject, made it possible for us to meet many of those who witnessed its beginnings, allowed a variety of critical approaches and specific themes within the general framework of the Congress, and facilitated the elucidation of ideas, doubts, and points of view that will certainly be pursued in more extensive investigations. The *Memorias* of this Congress will gather a great deal of material on a subject that until now has only been treated in isolated critical efforts. Our gratitude goes to Dr. Earle and his indefatigable assistant, Secretary General Germán Gullón, for this extremely fruitful Congress. Members and friends of the Institute await with great eagerness the two phases of the Eighteenth Congress, which will take place at the University of Florida at Gainesville and the University of Rio de Janeiro in Brazil, in 1977. ◯

1. The other members of the Board of Directors for the term 1973-75 are: Vice Presidents: Professors Donald Yates (Michigan State University) and Luis Sainz de Medrano (Universidad Complutense); Governors: Professors Angela B. Dellepiane (CUNY) and Seymour Menton (University of California, Irvine); Executive Secretary-Treasurer: Professor Julio Matas (University of Pittsburgh); Director of Publications: Alfredo A. Roggiano (University of Pittsburgh); Special Guest of the Board of Directors: Professor Emir Rodríguez Monegal (Yale University).
2. The other supporting organizations were The American Council of Learned Societies, and the Office of Inter-American Programs of the U.S. Department of State.